HOW TO

**FORGIVE**

WHEN

**IT FEELS**

**IMPOSSIBLE**

# HOW TO
# **FORGIVE**
# WHEN
# **IT FEELS**
# **IMPOSSIBLE**

## PETER HORROBIN

**Chosen**
*a division of Baker Publishing Group*
Minneapolis, Minnesota

Published by Chosen Books
11400 Hampshire Avenue South
Bloomington, Minnesota 55438
www.chosenbooks.com

Chosen Books is a division of
Baker Publishing Group, Grand Rapids, Michigan

Printed in the United States of America

ISBN 978-0-8007-9999-1

This edition published 2020.

Previously published in the United States under the title *The Most Powerful Prayer on Earth* by Regal Books.

Published in the United Kingdom as *Forgiveness—God's Master Key* by Sovereign World Ltd, Ellel Ministries International, Ellel, Lancaster, Lancashire, LA2 0HN, United Kingdom. (Previously titled *The Most Powerful Prayer on Earth*).

Cover design by Emily Weigel

20  21  22  23  24  25  26      7  6  5  4  3  2  1

# CONTENTS

*Jesus said, "Father, forgive them, for*
*they do not know what they are doing."*

*Luke 23:34*

# PREFACE

Since the first edition of this book was published, I have ministered in every continent. I have found that the principles this book contains are life transforming to every people group on the planet. There is no one that does not have a forgiveness issue that needs to be resolved.

Forgiveness truly is God's master key. It is the most powerful life-transforming tool that we have. It is not only the key to the restoration of our relationship with God, but it is also the key to healing from the consequences of hurtful and damaging human relationships.

From the cross Jesus prayed those dramatic words to God, "Father, forgive them, for they do not know what they are doing" (Luke 23:34). What an example He showed to us all about having a forgiving heart even when people do dreadfully bad things.

Learning to pray this most powerful of prayers is the beginning of a lifetime of adventures with God. It will not only bring healing to your past, but it will also open up new doors for you in the future. It is both God's master key and a key of miracles.

I know of many, many people whose lives have been transformed completely by God as they have lived out the results of praying this prayer. Some of their stories are in this book.

The first edition was simply called *The Most Powerful Prayer on Earth*. With added testimonies from some of those who have put the forgiveness prayer into practice, the title of this new edition now reflects the fact that so many have found it to be the master key they had been looking for. It is a master key that unlocks answers to the most difficult problems—even ones once thought impossible to resolve.

I can guarantee that if you learn how to pray this prayer sincerely from your heart, your life will never be the same. You will be changed, your circumstances will be changed, and you, too, will have a story to tell of what God has done in your life.

Without forgiveness as a foundation stone of our faith, every time we are hurt by what someone else says or does, we will be encased in yet more bondage. Forgiveness is the master key that opens the door of hope and healing.

I pray you will walk with me in this exciting adventure of faith. I will show you how to use the master key, and we will watch what God does in your life as a result!

# 1 A Master Key
## God's Way Out

A large house has many rooms and many doors. Each door has its own key. But a master key is designed to open any door in the building. The person with the master key can go anywhere.

The life we have is like a building with many different rooms. Each room contains the memories of important events in life. Some of the doors remain wide open, and we enjoy the memories these rooms contain. Other doors are closed, but we have no difficulty opening them whenever we wish. There is no pain associated with the memories these rooms contain.

But some of the doors are both closed and locked. What lies behind these doors is too painful to look at, and often the key has been thrown away. Some of these rooms have names such as trauma, rejection, betrayal, abuse, disloyalty, divorce or accidents.

People continue through life knowing there is unresolved pain behind these locked doors. Sometimes the pain was caused by others, and sometimes the pain was caused by their own mistakes. They often do not know how to resolve a situation for which they believe they are responsible. They do their very best to carry on, but as the years go by it gets harder and harder to cover up the fact that they are hurting.

The homes of some people have so many locked doors that there is very little space left in which to live. They have closed the doors on the mess inside hoping that the doors will stay shut forever. Because of all of these locked doors, however, the people cease to be able to function effectively as normal human beings. There can be so much hidden pain, trauma, anger, resentment or jealousy that they become less and less like the people God intended them to be.

Sometimes the mess on the inside seeps out from under the doors of the locked rooms. When that happens, people try to cover the mess up and carry on as if nothing is happening. But everyone else can see the mess, and those with whom they are in relationship have to live with the consequences.

Sometimes they try to clean up the mess from the outside; however, a point will be reached where the mess coming from under the doors is more than they can cope with. They know that they can only deal with the problem properly by opening the door and going inside. In some cases, the key has been thrown away. They cannot open the doors by themselves, and they need help. They need a new key.

Amazingly, Jesus left us a master key—a key so powerful and effective that it can open even the most stubborn of these locked doors. But He requires our cooperation to use it.

Jesus is not frightened of the mess that lies behind the doors. He wants to go in with us and help us clean it up. He designed this master key personally for you and for me, and then He showed us how to use it.

This golden master key is the most powerful prayer on earth. It is life transforming. As you hold this book, you are holding the instructions on how to use it. No circumstance is so awful or devastating that it is beyond the relevance of this amazing prayer.

Hannah was on a fast track to drugs and suicide. Her life had been ruined by years of cruel and painful sexual abuse in her family. She placed the master key in the door and prayed the prayer. God changed her life forever.

Michael was in despair because the wife he had loved so much had fallen for his best friend and walked out on him. When he prayed the prayer, his broken heart was healed, and he was able to start again and rebuild his life.

Lynda had lost hope. In her twenties, she was on a lifetime disability pension following a terrible accident. She prayed the prayer, and now she is married and living a normal life—no disability and no need for a pension.

Your circumstances might not be as bad as Hannah's, Michael's or Lynda's—or they might be worse. Whatever your circumstances are, when you learn to pray the most powerful prayer on earth from your heart, things will change. They will change because you, who have always been part of your circumstances, will also be changed.

Read on and learn how to use this wonderful life transforming master key.

# 2 The Most Powerful Prayer on Earth

## Spiritual Dynamite

Jesus not only taught us how to pray, but He also taught us how to use spiritual dynamite. Toward the end of His life He found Himself in an impossible situation. There was no way out. What was He going to do?

### The Prayer That Jesus Prayed

After three wonderful years of teaching and healing people, the tables were turned against Jesus. He was now facing crucifixion (see Luke 23). Many different people had played a part in the unfolding scenario that led to His present situation.

First, there were the religious leaders. They were jealous of Jesus' popularity and threatened by His power and authority. They hated Him.

Next, there was Judas—the deluded disciple who thought that thirty pieces of silver was a fair price to betray his master. He committed suicide eventually.

Pilate also played a role at Jesus' trial. He was the weak-willed governor of the Roman province of Judea who tried to wash his hands of any responsibility for what was happening.

And then there was Herod, the powerless Jewish king to whom Pilate sent Jesus for a second opinion. Herod only ridiculed and mocked Jesus. The chief priests and the teachers of the Law watched the performance and accused Him vehemently.

A large crowd of visitors were in Jerusalem for the Passover Feast. Urged on by the authorities, they were incited to clamor for Jesus' execution. They demanded insistently, "Crucify him! Crucify him!" (Luke 23:21).

And let's not forget Barabbas, the notorious criminal who gained his freedom at the expense of Jesus' life.

The Roman soldiers were at Jesus' arrest and crucifixion. They were obeying the orders of their commanding officer as they drove the nails through Jesus' body and into the cross. They cast lots for His clothes and mocked Him with cruel words. "If you are the king of the Jews, save yourself" (Luke 23:37).

And finally, you and I were there, alongside of every other human being there has ever been.

All of these people, including you and I, were responsible for Jesus being led out to Calvary to be crucified. He met His death alongside two common criminals who were scheduled for execution on the same day.

In the beginning, humankind turned its back on God and broke relationship with Him. As a result, death entered into the human race. It was our sin, therefore, that caused the Father to put the only possible rescue plan into effect that could restore the broken relationship between God and humankind. God loved the world so much that He gave His only Son to pay the ultimate price for our sin—Jesus' death on a cross. Our sin took Jesus there. Jesus' love kept Him there.

There is no one else who has ever walked the face of this earth who suffered such terrible injustice. No one else has ever had a greater excuse to blame others and cry out, "Not fair."

What did Jesus do? He prayed. And this is what He prayed: "Father, forgive them, for they do not know what they are doing" (Luke 23:34). I believe this is the single most powerful prayer that has ever been prayed. Not only did Jesus walk in personal forgiveness toward all of those who were the agents of His suffering, but He also asked God to forgive them.

To ask God to forgive in circumstances such as this was an extraordinary demonstration of what Jesus meant when He said, "Bless those who curse you, pray for those who mistreat you" (Luke 6:28 NASB). Jesus asked His Father to allow those who had persecuted Him to enter into the wonderful benefits that He had planned and purposed for them, benefits such as joy, release from bondage and the greatest of all, a relationship with Him.

All the angels of heaven must have bowed in silent wonder as they saw their beloved Jesus turn His back on resentment, bitterness, anger and revenge as He asked the Father to forgive all of those who had contributed to His death. What a man. What a God.

## The Need for a Forgiving Heart

It is impossible to ask God to forgive those who have hurt us without first forgiving them ourselves. Jesus even said that if we do not forgive those who have hurt us, then our Father in heaven will not forgive us (see Matthew 6:15).

People are often surprised to find that this is in the Bible. Surely God wants to forgive us. He does, but He has also given us a choice, and He will not override the choices we make. If we choose not to forgive those who have hurt us, we put ourselves under their control. If we are under their control, we cannot be free for God to heal us and set us free. If Jesus had not forgiven all those who had hurt Him, that lack of forgiveness would have changed His relationship with Father God.

When we confess our sin to God but refuse to forgive others, we are asking God to do something for us that we are not willing to do for others. That is hypocrisy.

Jesus told a parable about a servant who was forgiven a massive debt of millions of dollars by his king, but this same servant refused to write off a tiny debt of a few dollars from his neighbor. When the king found out about this, he threw the servant into prison until he could repay the entire amount. Jesus warned that those who behave like the servant will never know freedom (see Matthew 18:23–35).

Jesus even told us to love our enemies. He knew that if we react in bitterness against those who oppose us and who do bad things to us, we will be in bondage to those people for as long as we live. He also knew that if we ignore this vital principle, we will find that our reaction to what others have done to us could do us as much harm as the original offense. He wanted us to be free from all that.

Only when we have truly forgiven others will we be able to pray Jesus' prayer, "Father, forgive them," from the heart. Forgiveness of others is the huge first step that leads to our total release from the chains that surround our hurting hearts.

## Change from the Inside Out

I was teaching at a conference in Hungary just as the communist walls in Russia and Eastern Europe were falling down and the last Russian tanks were leaving Budapest. The people who had come to the conference were from the surrounding Communist-controlled nations.

As I looked at this large body of severely oppressed Christians, my heart went out to them. I felt a portion of the grief that God must have felt because of all they had suffered. Many were still suffering physically. Their physical disposition reflected their internal pain.

I took a huge risk and talked to them about forgiving their Communist oppressors. I did not know how they would respond, but the Spirit of God changed them as they began to understand what Jesus said about forgiving their enemies.

One by one people began to stand up as they made the choice to forgive. Then suddenly, they were all standing! Through the translator, I led them in a prayer. Phrase by phrase they spoke out their forgiveness.

The Spirit of God fell upon the people in the very hall where Communist leaders had previously met for their conferences. I spoke out that Jesus had come to set the captives free (see Luke 4:18), and then I took authority over the powers of darkness that were holding these people in bondage.

Healing began to flow from Father God into His hurting people. They were changing on the inside. In a short period of time, their bodies began to reflect the deep inner healing they were experiencing. I watched miracles take place before my very eyes. People were walking taller as bent and hurting backs were restored through forgiveness.

Never in all my years of ministering healing to people around the world have I seen God do this much healing among so many people in such a short space of time. As the people forgave their oppressors, they experienced firsthand the wonderful power of God that is liberated through the simple act of forgiveness from the heart.

## The Power of the Prayer

"Father, forgive them" is the most powerful prayer that you can ever pray.

- It transforms your relationship with God.
- It releases the power of the Holy Spirit into your life.
- It restores your soul.
- It opens the door to God's healing.
- It transforms your relationships with others.

But none of us can truly pray this extraordinary prayer until we have learned to forgive others for what they have done to us. And sometimes, we need to forgive ourselves before we are able to turn our hearts toward blessing other people.

Stephen, the first Christian martyr, learned the lesson of forgiveness well. He had such a forgiving attitude toward his accusers that when he was stoned to death—with the man who became the apostle Paul watching on—he, too, was able to pray the most powerful prayer on earth. With words very similar to those Jesus had used, he prayed, "Lord, do not hold this sin against them" (Acts 7:60).

How important it is that we learn to live like this in the ordinary circumstances of life and not just when we are facing the extremes of persecution that Stephen and countless others have faced through the centuries.

Learning to pray this amazing prayer from your heart could be the most important thing you will ever do. It is God's master key, specially designed to unlock the most stubborn problems in your life.

It is the spiritual dynamite that God uses to blow apart the prison doors—the doors that can keep us locked in the pain of the past. It is the most powerful prayer on earth.

# 3 Forgive and Be Forgiven

## God's Divine Law of Blessing

Every day people exceed the speed limit in their cars. They break the law of the land in which they live. But unless they are caught by the police, nothing happens. Laws such as this are man-made, and men are needed to enforce them.

### The Laws of the Universe

There are other laws in the universe, however, that are not man-made. If we ignore these laws, there are consequences even if there is no one there to enforce them. These laws are both physical and spiritual.

Take, for example, the law of gravity. If you drop a coin, it falls to the floor. If you step off a cliff your body will obey the law of gravity. You will fall downward, probably to your death. Everything in the universe obeys the law of gravity. No one can ignore it—not even for a moment. Nothing and no one can ever change it.

There are many other physical laws that control the whole of the physical universe. All of them are unchangeable. They are a reflection both of the unchangeable character of creator God and of the order He built into the universe.

The early pioneers of science focused their attention on discovering these laws. Without such laws and the order that they bring, the physical universe would be nothing but chaos. Life would be impossible, and human beings could not survive. Men and women are physical beings who are subject to these physical laws.

There is more to a human being, however, than just having a physical body. Humans are also spiritual beings. Not only is the shape and design of the human body unique, but the human character and personality are also totally unique. The Bible uses words such as *soul* and *spirit* to describe this spiritual nature (see Psalm 35:9, 51:10; 1 Thessalonians 5:23; Hebrews 4:12).

We are both physical and spiritual beings. Because we are physical, we are subject to the laws of the physical universe. But because we are spiritual, we are subject to the spiritual laws that God has built into the spiritual universe.

And because we live at the interface between the physical and spiritual worlds, what happens in the physical can affect the spiritual, and what happens in the spiritual can also affect the physical.

As children we learn quickly about the dangers of ignoring physical laws. Our parents try to protect us from experiencing the law of gravity by urging us to be cautious around stairs, and they teach us the laws of motion by keeping us away from dangerous traffic.

But where do we learn about the dangers of ignoring spiritual laws?

It was God's intention that our parents should not only teach us vital physical lessons, but they should also teach us vital spiritual lessons. For just as there can be very serious physical consequences from being ignorant of the physical laws, there are consequences even more serious that result from being ignorant of the spiritual laws. Ignoring physical laws have serious consequences in present time, but ignoring spiritual laws can also have serious eternal consequences.

Because you and I—and all humankind—chose to rebel against the God who made us, relationship with Him was broken. As a result, we lost the understanding of these spiritual principles that we would otherwise have understood naturally.

But God loved us so much that He did two things to help us. First, He gave us His written Word (the Bible) so that we could understand about spiritual things and learn what the consequences are of ignoring spiritual laws. Second,

He sent His Son, Jesus (the Living Word), so that we could have a restored relationship with Him.

Jesus tells us that one of the reasons He came was to show us what Father God is really like, for He and the Father are one. He told His disciples that if they had seen Him, they had also seen the Father (see John 14:7–9).

## The Law of Forgiveness

Every one of us has free will—the ability to make choices about anything and everything in life. We can make right or wrong choices, good or bad choices. The right and good choices will bring blessing into our lives. The wrong and bad choices will have the opposite effect.

This brings us right back to the most powerful prayer on earth. To pray this amazing prayer, it is necessary that we embrace a principle that is at the heart of God's spiritual laws. Make the right choice concerning this principle, and you are headed for blessing.

The disciples asked Jesus how to pray. His answer was to give them a pattern that would form the basis of all our prayers. We call it the Lord's Prayer (see Matthew 6:9–13; Luke 11:1–4).

All who believe in God want to know that their sins are forgiven. They do not want their unforgiven sins to remain on God's slate for eternity and create a barrier between them and God. Therefore, it would have been a relief to the disciples to hear Jesus include within the Lord's Prayer the phrase that began, "Forgive us our debts" (Matthew 6:12).

We trespass when we go beyond what we are allowed. If we ignore the signs that say *Private* and walk on someone else's land, we are trespassing. When we step over God's line that divides what is right from what is wrong, we are trespassing against God. We leave behind our spiritual footprints, and God knows where we have been.

Just as human relationships are damaged when we trespass on someone else's property, our relationship with God is damaged when we trespass spiritually. Our conscience is affected, and we know we have done wrong.

Deep inside we long for relational restoration. To deal with the situation, we need to face up to our pride and come back to God humbly. We need to say we are sorry and ask for forgiveness for our sin. Humility is the gateway to God's grace. The Lord's Prayer brings us to this point of asking God for forgiveness.

We find, however, that the next phrase contains some unwelcome and challenging words. Not only does it say, "Forgive us our debts," but it also says, "as we also have forgiven our debtors" (Matthew 6:12). It is here that we come up against one of those vital spiritual laws—laws that cannot be changed, and laws that we are subject to even though we do not want to be.

The disciples must have struggled with the idea of having to forgive others as well, for Jesus had to tell them again—and in very simple words: "If you do not forgive others their sins, your Father will not forgive your sins" (Matthew 6:15).

Peter, one of Jesus' disciples, even asked Jesus how often he needed to forgive others, suggesting that perhaps seven was a very large and generous number. There was a gentle rebuke in Jesus' words when He replied, "Not seven times, Peter, but seventy times seven" (see Matthew 18:21–22). In other words, stop counting and just keep on forgiving.

## The Law of Blessing

If we want to know the continuous blessing of God, then we have to forgive others continuously and quickly. Otherwise when we ask God to forgive us, we will be asking Him for something that we are not willing to give to others. We will become trapped by our own hypocrisy.

There is no way that Jesus could have prayed the most powerful prayer on earth if He had not first come to the point of forgiving those who nailed Him to that piece of wood. He knew that forgiveness of others was an essential gateway to knowing the continuous blessing of God. This is what He had taught His disciples to do time and time again.

Forgiveness of sin is the greatest possible blessing that God makes available to His children. But if we are not willing to forgive others, we will miss out on God's best for our lives.

Consider the examples of Mary and Alec who discovered the blessing that comes with forgiveness. Mary had been abused sexually by her father for many years, and she had also done many wrong things, including having had several wrong sexual relationships. In the arms of other men, she was looking for the comfort her father should have given her.

Mary knew these relationships had been wrong, and with many tears, she confessed them to God. She knew she had done the right thing in confessing them, but she did not feel much different as a result. She could not understand why.

It was then that she had to face the hardest decision of her life—whether or not she would choose to forgive her own father. How could she, after he had done such terrible things to her? But deep inside she knew that it was her attitude toward her father that was the barrier preventing her from knowing the forgiveness of God for herself.

Slowly, Mary faced the issue. She realized that if she did not forgive her father, the memories of what he had done would control her for the rest of her life. She wanted very much to be free, and yet to be so, she had to give up all of the bitterness and anger in her heart.

Finally, the battle was won, and she was able to forgive him. It was only as God lifted the burden of her sins that she realized the full depth of His love for her. She experienced the blessing of God in a totally new way—just as Jesus had said, "For if you forgive other people when they sin against you, your heavenly Father will also forgive you" (Matthew 6:14).

Mary had learned that we cannot ignore God's spiritual law of forgiveness. It is just as powerful in the spiritual realm as the law of gravity is in the physical realm. Ignore the law and we bring suffering on ourselves; abide by the law and we walk in God's blessing.

Alec had struggled desperately with what he had thought was the unfairness of having to forgive others—until he experienced the joy and blessing of forgiving the one person who had hurt him the most.

Just like Mary, Alec was still carrying scars from his father. His scars were not the scars of sexual abuse, however, but of having been squeezed into a career mold. His father had pressured him into being a doctor, which was a career that did not match his gifts, abilities and desires. In midlife he went into deep depression and had to retire early from his work as a family doctor.

When he decided to forgive, it was as if the black clouds of depression that had masked every activity of his life lifted from his mind. He became a totally different man. As he started to rediscover himself, he was desperate to think of anyone else he could forgive! He wanted to enjoy more of God's blessing on his life.

Mary and Alec, and thousands of others like them, discovered God's spiritual laws the hard way. By ignoring the command of God to forgive, they discovered the law that bound them in spiritual chains. When they forgave, they discovered another law—this time a law of blessing. They began to know the forgiveness of God for themselves. They learned the relationship between forgiving others and being forgiven, and they began to taste for themselves the blessings that God promises.

# 4 But They Do Not Deserve It!

## The Biggest Obstacle

It is true that when people do bad things that hurt others they do not deserve to be forgiven. Jesus could have had this perspective with everyone who was involved in the events that led up to Calvary, from the crowds who shouted, "Crucify Him!" to the soldiers who drove the nails through His hands. He would have been right—they did not deserve to be forgiven.

But instead, He cried out to God saying, "Father, forgive them, for they do not know what they are doing" (Luke 23:34).

Forgiveness does not seem to make any sense. It especially does not make sense when we are hurting deeply because of what others have done to us. A sense of injustice rises up from within and shouts out, "It's not fair!"

Forgiveness does not make sense—until we understand that forgiveness is always an act of love and never an act of justice. It is important that we understand the difference between forgiveness and justice.

## The Demand for Justice

When a man is arrested for stealing, justice requires that he pay for the crime by returning what has been stolen to its rightful owner, by spending time in jail or by paying a fine. The Bible makes this point very clearly when it describes some of the punishments that were appropriate for particular crimes. Justice had to be done.

When the debt to society has been paid, a former criminal is said to be a free man. But is he? That depends on how we look at things. As far as society is concerned, the man is free to go about his legitimate affairs. As long as his behavior remains within the boundaries of the law, he will remain a free man for the rest of his days.

Real freedom for the criminal, however, can only come when he also says sorry for what he has done to the person he has wronged, when he receives forgiveness and when he does everything he can do to make restitution for his crime.

This still only deals with the human consequences of the man's sin. In reality, not only has he done wrong against the victim of his crime and against society, but he has also broken one of God's commandments and come up against one of God's spiritual laws. He can make it right with society and the person he has stolen from, but can he ever make it right with God?

We have already established that we have both physical and spiritual elements to us and that there are spiritual consequences for the physical things we do. When we do wrong, our relationship with God is damaged and, as a result, we wrap ourselves in spiritual chains. No one needs to put us in a spiritual prison for what we have done—we are already there.

It is a bit like gravity. In the physical realm, once we step off the edge of a cliff, we do not have any choice about whether or not we will fall. We will fall downward whether we like it or not.

In the same way, when we choose to rebel against God and we ignore the spiritual laws that He has built into the spiritual universe, we will fall into a prison created by our own choices.

Once we have stepped off the spiritual cliff, it is too late. We will find ourselves in a prison from which there is no obvious way out. Just as human justice requires that the price of crime must be paid, eternal justice requires that the price of sin must also be paid.

But if, for example, you have been put in a physical prison because you cannot pay the fine that has been demanded by the judge, there is no way that you can get out and earn the money required. You are in an impossible situation. You do not have the money to pay the fine, and you cannot get out of prison to earn money until the fine has been paid. This situation requires someone who is not in prison to come and pay the fine.

Because of sin, every human being who has ever walked the face of this earth is in the same prison. We have all walked off the edge of the same spiritual cliff and discovered that spiritual gravity is as unchangeable as physical gravity. Our relationship with God has been broken, and we are in jail. And what is more, there is no other living human who is able to pay the fine and meet the requirements of justice. We are all trapped in the same prison.

Jesus, however, is the one exception. He is the only human being who never sinned and could never, therefore, have had a reason for being put in jail. Jesus was the completely sinless Son of God who came to earth as a human being. He was tempted, but He never sinned. Jesus never allowed Himself to come under the control of others. He never stepped off the edge of the spiritual cliff to discover the consequences of spiritual gravity. And He always made the right choices, never ending up in the spiritual prison that has entrapped every other human being.

As a sinless human being, Jesus was in a position to plead the case of sinners and to pay the price for those in jail. The ultimate price for sin is a broken relationship with God— in other words, death.

Because Jesus had never sinned, He was not in prison with us. When He paid the price of our sin through dying on the cross, there was no crime attached to His record, and the jailer could not keep Him in prison. Even death could not control Him (see Acts 2:24).

It was as if He went to prison on our behalf and paid the fine that we each deserved to pay. Justice was done. He became united to the whole of the human race through His death. He knew what it was like to feel forsaken by God the Father, but because He was otherwise a free man, death could not keep Him bound. The resurrection was a certain next step. It was a matter of when—not if—it would happen.

Through the death of Jesus, the price for sin was paid and justice was done. God made a way for the spiritual (eternal) consequences of human sin to be dealt with.

## Peace with God

Unconfessed and unforgiven sin has a habit of working away at us on the inside. What begins as a spiritual problem can, in time, become a physical problem. When Jesus healed a paralyzed man, He first dealt with forgiveness of the man's sins. James tells us that we need to confess our sins to one another so that we will be healed (see James 5:16).

The following story of Tania illustrates the peace that confession brings. At the end of a conference session in which I was teaching about healing, Tania came up to me and confessed that she had been embezzling money from her employer and now owed him thousands of dollars. The knowledge of what she had done was crippling her on the inside. The stolen money had not brought her the pleasure she had anticipated.

As she poured out her confession to God, she knew that her only way forward was to confess her sin to her employer and make restitution. She went away that night full of apprehension about what was going to happen in the office the next day, but she also went away at peace with God for the first time since she had started stealing the money. Her healing had begun.

In the example we used earlier, a criminal who has been arrested for stealing is not completely free, even when he deals with the human consequences of his crime. What should he do in order to be totally free? All that remains is for him to trust Jesus as His Savior and ask God to forgive him for his sins.

None of us deserves such generous treatment. We do not deserve to be forgiven for anything we have done. Forgiveness is only possible because God is a God of love. Jesus paid the price willingly, thus ensuring that in the courts of heaven justice had been done.

It is certainly true that our criminal does not deserve to be forgiven. The sad fact is, though, that neither do you or I. Ultimately, we are all guilty of the same crime—rebellion against a holy God. We have all landed in the same jail.

Or to use a different analogy, we are all in the same boat. Yes, some people may do things that are much worse than others, but the spiritual and eternal consequences are just the same.

## The Freedom of Forgiveness

A similar principle operates with respect to forgiveness. Regardless of whether what has been done to you is large or small, the end result of unforgiveness is the same. When we choose not to forgive someone, bitterness, resentment and anger build up and take root inside us. They act like cancers on our emotions, and we get all knotted up inside—no matter how much in the right we may think we are or how much in the wrong the other person may have been.

We can make comparisons between us and them; we can elevate ourselves to a place of superiority, or we can justify our lack of forgiveness to others on the grounds that we are much better than they are. In reality, however, it does not help us at all.

It may be true that the people who have really hurt us have sinned against us to a much greater degree than we could ever have done to them. But that does not minimize the effect that sin has internally on us.

As a result of our unforgiveness, the offense we have already suffered continues to grow daily to the point that it becomes all consuming. Our true selves become lost in a sea of resentment that can lead to years of negative emotional, psychological and even physical conditions (see Hebrews 12:15).

If you want to be free from the poison of bitterness and healed of the devastating consequences that unforgiveness can have on your health, your family and all of your relationships, then you need to make a choice to start forgiving now. Only then will you be able to follow Jesus' example to pray "Father, forgive them."

When you have reached the place of being able to ask God to forgive those who have hurt you, the chains of bondage will begin to fall away, and you will be able to walk free at last.

Jenny's story illustrates the freedom that forgiveness brings. Jenny had suffered unspeakable things at the hands of her mother. Thirty years later, Jenny's life was only sustainable through high doses of medication that were prescribed by her psychiatrist. Her whole life was in the balance. Suicide seemed an attractive way out.

In reality, although there had been no relationship with her mother for many years, she was still controlled by her mother's acts of abuse. The chains of unforgiveness kept all of her memories and the suffering that she experienced during childhood fresh in her mind. She was trapped.

Forgiving her mother seemed like the most dangerous and unfair walk Jenny could ever go on. It felt like an impossible journey. But little by little Jenny took the steps and walked away from the pain of the past. She began with the small things and then progressed step by step to the really big things that had devastated her childhood and subsequently ruined her life. It took quite a while before she could face the reality of all that had happened to her. But because she was willing, the Lord helped her, and she got to the point where she could forgive.

The chains of bondage were broken, and Jenny is now free to be herself for the first time in her life. Forgiving her mother began the process of personal healing from the pain of the past. Praying that God would bless her mother meant that Jenny would stay free in the future.

Jenny's mother did not deserve to be forgiven, but not forgiving her was condemning Jenny to hell on earth. Learning to pray the most powerful prayer on earth set Jenny free forever.

# 5 Starting with Parents

## The Importance of Forgiving Our Parents for Everything

Whether you like it or not, your parents are still the most important people in your life. They contributed more to who and what you are than anyone else. And that is the case even if you were placed for adoption.

Contrary to what those who promote abortion tell us about aborted babies, you were a human being from the moment of your conception. For that reason, even the circumstances of that most momentous occasion of your life could be having an effect on you now.

On one hand, this earliest influence from your parents could have provided you with the most wonderful start to life, surrounding you with loving care and tenderness. On the other hand, if your mother was raped by an intruder, it could have been the most horrific traumatic experience. Most people began life somewhere in between these two extremes.

## Facing Our Inheritance

Even if you had the most loving start to life and were a baby who was very wanted, your parents were still a long way from being perfect. They inherited the consequences of their own parents' inadequacies and upbringing, and their parents inherited consequences from the previous generation, and so on. All of us are the fruit of our ancestors, and not everything we have inherited from them is good.

This may sound like bad news, and you may ask, "What's the point of telling me all this when there is absolutely nothing I can do to change what happened in the past?" I agree that if there were really nothing you could do, then sharing that information would be cruel. It would create unnecessary anger and make whatever problems you have seem even worse.

It is true that you cannot change the influence that your great-grandparents had on your grandparents, or the influence your grandparents had on your parents. It is also true that you cannot go back in time and change the circumstances of your own conception. Neither can you change anything that happened during those vital nine months in your mother's womb, or what happened during the dangerous journey from the security of the womb into the arms of the midwife or doctor on the day you were born.

Your early childhood and nurturing were also outside of your control. All you could do was receive what was offered, be it good or bad. Whatever early schooling you had was not your choice. All your early education was organized by others, and you had to either enjoy or endure the schooling your parents provided for you. In fact, it probably was not until your teenage years that you began to make your own choices about the things that really mattered to you in life.

But by the time you got to the place of making responsible adult decisions, you may already have experienced trauma as a result of the weaknesses and wrong choices of your parents. When your turn came to make choices for yourself, you most likely began to repeat the same sort of mistakes they did. You probably even made some new mistakes of your own. These new mistakes add to the burden you will pass on to your own children.

"What a mess," I hear you saying. I agree! What is the point of even knowing all this? The point is that while you cannot change anything of the inheritance your parents left you, God can change you right now if you give Him a chance. You do not have to continue to suffer the ongoing consequences.

## Cutting the Chains

In the first chapter we talked about how there are many different rooms in the house of your life. For most people, the bad memories of parental problems are placed behind closed doors. People believe that they have been locked away forever. They try to make the best of what life has offered them without realizing that there is a master key to all those rooms and that God can clean up the mess that is on the other side of the doors.

God will not change the facts of what happened in your past, but He can change you in the present so that you need not have to endure the consequences of those things for the rest of your days.

The master key to it all is forgiveness. Without using this key, those doors will never be opened. And unless those rooms are cleaned out, the poison that lies behind the locked doors will never stop seeping out into the remainder of your life.

By using the key of forgiveness, you can walk away from the past. With this key and with God's help, you can start again. Your parents really did not know what the consequences could be of their mistakes. It was impossible for them to comprehend that what they were doing could cause you such problems.

The Bible puts it this way: "Our ancestors sinned, but now they are gone, and we are suffering for their sins" (Lamentations 5:7 GNT). This reality is also expressed clearly within the Ten Commandments (see Exodus 20:5). This seems very unfair until we realize that God's original intention was that children would be influenced for good by the good things that come down to them from their parents, grandparents and even great-grandparents (see Exodus 20:6). Just as a rainwater pipe is equally effective for carrying clean or dirty water, the channel that God created to bless the family line can be used to either carry the consequences of the sins of humankind (because of the Fall) or blessings.

We need to thank God for all the good things that have come to us from our parents and ancestors and begin the work of forgiving them for everything that has come to us that has acted as a curse on our lives. As we do this, chains that are holding us in bondage to the past will be broken, and we can start to become the people God intended us to be.

## Setting Ourselves Free

In the story *Gulliver's Travels*, Jonathan Swift tells us how Gulliver ends up in Lilliput, the country of tiny people. The people there find this "giant" fast asleep and wonder how they can protect themselves from him when he wakes up.

What they did was tie him down with thousands of strands of rope. To Gulliver, however, the rope was small enough that it was like fine cotton. Any one of those strands could have been snapped in a fraction of a second with minimum effort. But because there were so many of them, he was held tight. When he woke up, he was unable to move.

Most of the things from our past that hold us down are like strands of fine cotton. Though each one has little power on its own, often there are so many that together they cripple us.

The most powerful prayer on earth asks us simply to say, "Father, forgive them. They didn't know what they were doing." For some people, this is an easy prayer to pray in respect to our parents and ancestors. We can understand that since they could not have known of our existence, they could not possibly have known what effect their behavior was going to have on us.

For other people, this is a really hard prayer. Because they see so many problems that have come to them from their parents, they have become very angry. Bitterness has taken root inside them, and the last thing they want to do is to forgive the people who have caused them such pain and heartache.

Consider the story of one lady who was struggling with rapidly developing arthritis in her joints. She could no longer dance and enjoy life. Her mother had also been a severe arthritic before she died. As the woman spoke out forgiveness to her parents and to everyone in her family line who had done things that had hurt her, God began to change her from the inside out.

It was not long before the pain and the arthritis in her joints had disappeared, and she was able to dance again. It was only a small step that she took—to pray, "Father, forgive them"—but that step took her a giant leap forward in both understanding and healing.

Why not spend a little while thinking about your parents and thanking God for all the good things that came to you through them? Then you can begin to forgive them and your ancestors for everything they have said or done that has had a negative effect on your life.

It may take quite a long time to work through all your feelings, but every time you forgive someone for something new, one of the strands that is holding you prisoner is being cut. Little by little you are setting yourself free from the chains of your past.

As you pray the most powerful prayer on earth, God is able to put new strength back into your life and take you a step nearer to fulfilling the destiny He has for you.

# Dealing with Thieves and Robbers

## Freedom from Those Who Have Stolen Part of Our Lives

Losses occur when thieves and robbers steal things that do not belong to them. When ordinary things such as cash, a camera or a computer are stolen from us, we lose the monetary value of those items.

In addition to this monetary value, we also lose the special added value attached to certain items. Most of us have items that hold great personal significance for us or our family—items such as a family heirloom, photographs, a much-loved car, a favorite piece of jewelry or something very personal that could have little or no monetary value but is utterly precious to us.

Such losses can be a very powerful source of personal pain. If they are not dealt with by forgiving the offenders and praying the most powerful prayer on earth, we will always end up in bitterness, anger and even fear of what else people might take.

When something is stolen from us, it is as if there is a strand of invisible rope stretching out from us to the thief. It is unforgiveness that holds each strand of the rope in place. Unforgiveness is like spiritual superglue—it acts instantly and sticks forever.

We could easily shake off the limiting effect of one such strand, but when there are many strands, they join together to make a rope that limits us. The rope can influence or even control every aspect of our lives. And every time we think about the person who did these things to us and we reinforce our feelings of bitterness and resentment through further expressions of unforgiveness, we strengthen the rope and add more superglue to its fixing.

This process can be passed down the generational line with one generation after another nursing a grudge of hatred and unforgiveness against the culprits and their descendants. Even today, for example, there are descendants of the MacDonald family from Scotland who only very reluctantly would have anything to do with a member of the Campbell family. This is due to what the Campbells did several hundred years ago in the terrible massacre of Glencoe.

The more we find security in our possessions, the more difficult it is to forgive those who have taken precious things from us. But in reality, there are things that are much more valuable in life than our possessions, and we need to get to a place in our relationship with God where our ultimate security is in Him, not in the property we own.

## I Have Been Robbed!

However important our possessions may be to us and however hard it may be to forgive someone who has robbed us of them, the effect of the loss is nowhere near as great as the loss caused by a completely different kind of theft. Most possessions can be replaced, but the category we are going to discuss can never be replaced. The effects of their loss can only be healed.

What I am referring to are things like character, reputation, identity, sexuality, time, health, children and family. We will look at just four of these as examples of the many ways you could be robbed of significant things in your life—your reputation, your sexuality, your time and your health.

The pain of having these things stolen is far greater and more consequential than the loss of any mere possessions. The remedy for being healed, however, is exactly the same as for the theft of our possessions—the most powerful prayer on earth.

## Reputation

Unkind and untrue words spoken about us by others have a habit of being passed around as gossip. By the time the stories have gone their rounds, and sometimes been added to by people in the chain, everyone who has heard and believed them has lowered their opinion of us. Something of our reputation has been stolen.

When people put such words in print, or perhaps release them on the internet, the effect is even more serious. They are now in a permanent format and can be read for as long as copies of the words are available.

Many years ago, certain people said and wrote totally untrue words about me and the ministry in which I am involved. Even today I come across people whose first instinct is to have nothing to do with this ministry because of the words that are lodged in their memory.

The laws of most countries have provisions to protect the good name of individuals from such slander and libel. Not only is it a serious legal offense in society to steal someone's good name, but it is also a very serious offense before God (see Exodus 20:16; Proverbs 19:5; Matthew 15:19).

The fact that what they were doing is wrong, however, does not give me an excuse to harbor bitterness against such thieves in my own heart. By doing so, I would only make it harder for people to find out the truth and change their opinion. Each time I come across someone who has been affected negatively by the words people have said or written about me is a fresh opportunity to forgive them and pray the most powerful prayer on earth. Ultimately, truth will be revealed, and God has to be the vindicator of our reputations.

Jesus suffered in this way, therefore we should not be surprised if it happens to us. How can it be that someone who did much good, healed many people and taught many wonderful truths could become the victim of so many false accusations from false witnesses and a braying crowd that cried out to the authorities for His blood?

People stole His reputation. They did Him a terrible disservice. But "Father, forgive them" was ultimately all that Jesus said. He could only have prayed this prayer if His heart was forgiving toward those who had hurt Him.

Jesus was given a marvelous opportunity to defend His reputation when Pilate, the Roman governor, asked Him to explain who He was. But Jesus chose not to answer the question. Instead, He stood in silence before Pilate (see John 19:6–12).

Jesus may have been crucified on the strength of the false accusations of His accusers, but three days later it was God who vindicated Him. Everything they had said about Jesus was demonstrated on resurrection morning to be untrue.

The only way to deal with those who try to steal your character and your reputation is to forgive them, to keep on doing what is right, to act with humility and integrity and to trust God with the outcome.

Sometimes even the opinions of your friends may be lowered because of what others say about you. That hurts, but you will suffer even more if you remain unforgiving in your heart. This can even have an effect on your health and your ability to function in the way God intended.

In this way, as you forgive those who speak or write wrong things about you, the spiritual superglue of unforgiveness will never get a chance to attach the ropes of bitterness to your heart.

### Sexuality

Abuse comes in many forms, such as physical or psychological abuse, but the form that has received a large amount of attention recently is sexual abuse.

Sexual abuse occurs when a sexual predator takes advantage of another human being in order to satisfy his or her perverted sexual desires and urges. This form of abuse can include the visual voyeurism of a peeping Tom, unwelcome sexual touching, sexual violence, rape or ritualistic sex. When it is all over, the abuser moves on to the next challenge without giving thought to the damage that has been done to the victim.

Men and women, boys and girls—all can be sexually abused, and the abuse can be either heterosexual or homosexual in nature. Whenever one person is forced unwillingly into some aspect of sexual activity against his or her will, abuse has taken place.

Sexuality is a wonderful gift from God that He intended to be enjoyed within the safe confines of an intimate marital relationship. Anything that deprives a person of his or her free will in the area of sexuality is a serious form of theft. When a woman is abused or raped, she is robbed of the intimate joy of giving herself freely to her husband. Each time the abuse takes place, more of the person is stolen.

God's plan for marriage is that both parties in the relationship will give something of themselves to the other. A beautiful and godly relationship is established through this God-ordained tie; however, when a person is forced to give himself or herself sexually, the bond that is created is very ungodly.

Even when forgiveness seems impossible, God can undo an ungodly tie and unscramble the mess. I have seen extraordinary healings take place in every culture of the world as people have brought the pain of such abuse to light, as they forgave the abusers and prayed the most powerful prayer on earth.

Forgiveness is the miracle key that allows God to undo the ties of abusive relationships and begin the work of healing and restoration. The past cannot be undone, but the future can be different as God heals the broken heart.

## Time

Each of us only has one life to live, and every available minute is a gift from God. Every minute matters, and we all get justifiably upset when someone robs us of time. But how would you react if someone placed you in prison unfairly for a crime you did not commit and then left you there for a generation?

Nelson Mandela spent close to thirty years in prison at the hands of the ruling white authorities in the Republic of South Africa. His crime? Opposing the cruel and abusive apartheid regime that robbed black communities of their right to land, resources and dignity as human beings.

He was robbed of a huge portion of his life. Few people have been robbed of so much time and yet been able to keep such a forgiving heart. He was released and vindicated and even became the first democratically elected president of South Africa.

In the latter stages of his life, he became an elder statesman on the world stage. He was given more stature than he could possibly have dreamed of during his years in prison. How did this happen? He turned the master key in the lock of personal bondage and lived out the results of praying the most powerful prayer on earth.

The chains of hatred were cut, and he walked free from his jail cell on Robben Island. Not only was he free physically, but he was also free from being isolated on an island of bitterness for the rest of his days.

## Health

Health and strength are prerequisites for the maximum enjoyment of all that life has to offer. But how do you cope when you are suddenly trapped in a damaged body that is the result of a terrible accident that was not your fault? The sense of loss and the pain of injustice are understandable and normal feelings.

I mentioned Lynda briefly in chapter one. Let me tell you more of her story. Lynda, who was only in her twenties, was on a night hike with other young people when she fell off a cliff into a ravine. She lay there for hours with her back broken before she was airlifted out.

She never should have fallen off that cliff. The leader of the hike had split off from the group, leaving them on a path headed for the edge of a cliff. The leader failed to warn the group of the danger—even though it was night. As Lynda tried to follow those ahead of her, she slipped off the edge and fell into open space.

For years she held unforgiveness for the man who should have led her to safety that night. She found herself disabled, on a pension for life and suffering constant pain and chronic fatigue. She was without hope of fulfilling any of her dreams. Career, marriage and all the fun of life lay devastated at the place where she fell.

She put the key in the lock, forgave the man who had been responsible for this devastation and opened the door of her life to the power of God. As we began to pray for her, there were many things that God did to bring about her healing. None of them could have happened if she had not first used the miracle key.

Today she is healed, no longer registered as disabled and married. She was willing to pray the most powerful prayer on earth, and the power of God to heal was released into her life. If Lynda had remained bitter and unforgiving, she would likely still be disabled and without hope of any real future because of the bitterness she had held on to.

---

One day, when Jim was a young boy, he was playing on a low roof. His dad said, "Jump into my arms." Jim jumped, but his dad purposefully stepped aside and let him land on the concrete. Jim's chest was crushed by the fall. Decades after that event, he was still an asthmatic. He had not been able to breathe properly since that terrible day in his early childhood.

When Jim forgave his dad, God opened the floodgates of healing. Years later, he is still healed completely of the asthma that had crippled his breathing.

Bad things and accidents happen every day. If something bad has happened to you and as a result you have been robbed of health and strength, have you ever thought about forgiving those who were responsible?

The effects of trauma on your health can be devastating, but refusing to forgive the people responsible will only make things worse. Choose to forgive them without condition, and the ropes of pain will be cut.

## It Is Time to Take Action!

There are many other ways that people can steal from you. Later, I will explain exactly what to do to be free of the pain of having these things stolen. But in case you want to start now to deal with some of the thieves and robbers, I recommend that you spend a few minutes thinking through your life and asking God to show you all the times that bad circumstances have robbed you. For each event, ask yourself honestly if there are people associated with those incidents you still need to forgive. Write down their names on a piece of paper. As you look at the list, remind yourself that these things are all in the past and that the only person who will continue to be hurt by them if you choose not to forgive is you.

Then express out loud your forgiveness to each person on the list. For some people, you might also want to pick up the phone or sit down and write them a letter. For others, such as a sexual abuser, this would be very inappropriate, since it could be seen by the abuser as a fresh opportunity to engage in an ungodly relationship.

Just do whatever you feel is necessary to wipe the slate clean between you and them. God will cut those chains and melt the superglue, and you will begin to walk free.

After you have expressed your forgiveness, shred or put a match to the piece of paper. As you do so, pray from your heart the most powerful prayer on earth: "Father, forgive them." It is all over!

# 7 Me Too?

## The Need to Forgive Ourselves

When talking about the mistakes of the past—and we have all made lots—many people begin their story with the words "I'll never forgive myself for . . ." There are some who have made the right choice to forgive, worked through the forgiveness process and faced all the emotions of what happened to them but still have one huge obstacle that remains in their healing process: themselves.

They manage to forgive everyone else under the sun, but somehow or other the guilt and burden of their own mistakes seem so huge that forgiving themselves has become an impossibility.

Sometimes when terrible mistakes have been made, often with very painful consequences, the sense of loss can be enormous. The mistake may have caused an awful accident that even led to the death of someone else. It may have been a relationship that should never have been pursued, a financial involvement that went wrong or any of a thousand other personal mistakes that could have been made with potentially lifelong consequences.

## It Is Up to You

It is true that the past cannot be changed, but it is also true that how you handle the future is in your hands. It is possible to learn vital lessons from the mistakes of the past, and those lessons might be a great blessing to you in the future.

Jesus died so that you would be forgiven. If you hold on to the personal guilt attached to these things and refuse to forgive yourself, you are almost saying that what Jesus did for you was not good enough.

If a child longs to receive some sweets from his daddy, but his fist is tightly clenched, he could receive nothing. By keeping his fist closed, he would have deprived himself of the goodies.

Often, people who refuse to forgive themselves yearn for God to heal them of all that has happened in the past. But they go to God with their spiritual fists closed. By their own choice, they forfeit many of the blessings that God longs to give.

## What Amazing Love!

Sometimes refusing to forgive yourself is choosing to punish yourself for what has happened. You do not believe that you deserve to be forgiven, so you hold yourself in personal condemnation. You make a choice to deprive yourself of life because you believe that is all you deserve. But that is not how God sees it.

Simon Peter, Jesus' disciple, went down this road. Three times he told people that he was not associated with Jesus because of fear of what might happen to him (see John 18:15–27). He betrayed Jesus by telling lies even though he loved Him so much that he could not bear the thought of not being as close to Him as possible when He was suffering.

Peter must have been filled with personal remorse at the terrible thing he had done. As a result, he did what many of us would have done—he withdrew to somewhere safe where he could indulge his self-pity. For Peter, that was in his boat fishing on the Sea of Galilee. But Jesus knew what Peter was going through.

After the resurrection, Jesus sought him out and asked him three times the very simple but profound question, "Do you love Me?" (see John 21:15–17). Jesus gave Peter the opportunity to tell Him that he loved Him for each of the times that he had betrayed Jesus.

For Simon Peter, this was probably the most important healing moment of his life. If Jesus had not sought him out, Peter would have probably spent the rest of his days rowing around the Sea of Galilee, wallowing in self-pity and wondering what might have been.

Like Peter, we all make mistakes. In this situation, the most important question for Jesus to ask was not "What did you do?" but "Do you love Me?" When we are open to receiving His love and expressing our own love in return, the healing power of God goes right into our hearts. God begins to heal us from the inside out. Love melts pain.

## All Wrapped Up

You may have forgiven other people and been freed of the control from others who have hurt you, but when you refuse God's love, you are still in bondage. You have substituted the bondage of control by others with a self-imposed bondage. You have wrapped yourself in so much self-condemnation that you are unable to function properly or relate normally with others.

There is a special service available at some airports for those who are worried that their suitcase may not make the journey in one piece. For a small fee, you can have your baggage encased completely in layer upon layer of tightly wrapped polyethylene. When the process is finished, the suitcase looks like a corpse wrapped in plastic graveclothes. There is no way that anything can come out or that anyone can get in.

One day as I watched these plastic-coated suitcases going around and around on the baggage carousel at London's Heathrow Airport, it crossed my mind that this is what people must look like when they refuse to forgive themselves. It is as if they are wrapped in spiritual plastic, and no one can get in or out.

Living in unforgiveness toward yourself will neither change your past nor improve your future. It will only limit your potential to fulfill the very best that God still has in store for you.

Yes, we do have to deal with the consequences of personal mistakes and sin. Relationships with both God and human beings need to be restored through confession and repentance. Restitution may also have to be made. But once these steps have been taken, we must learn to walk away from the mess and not keep on going back to wallow in the mud of our own mistakes.

Hippopotamuses can wallow deep in mud for days on end. They love it. It is part of their natural environment. People are capable of wallowing in their personal spiritual mud for a lifetime. But God did not intend for people to live like hippos. Mud is not our natural spiritual environment. We must leave the mud behind and enjoy living in the freedom that only living God's way can bring.

We need to forgive ourselves and pray the most powerful prayer on earth for ourselves, not just for other people.

# 8 How Often, Lord?

## Simon Peter's Most Important Lesson

Simon Peter had a problem. He knew what Jesus had taught about forgiveness, but like every other human being, he was struggling with it and was looking for a bit of common sense to prevail. Maybe there was a particular person Peter was having difficulty forgiving. Maybe he was looking for an excuse to hang on to a bit of unforgiveness.

*Surely there has to be a limit*, he must have thought. *You don't really expect me to keep on forgiving forever, do You? Especially when people keep on doing the same thing to me time and time again?*

Simon came up with his own answer to the problem and put it to Jesus as a proposal that he hoped would settle the matter once and for all. He was keen to get a ruling from Jesus as to what the limit was.

"How about seven times, Lord? Surely no one deserves to be forgiven more often than that?" (see Matthew 18:21).

## No Limits

I would love to have seen the gentle smile on Jesus' face. It is probable that when He answered the question, neither Peter nor the rest of the disciples was prepared for His challenging answer.

"Not seven times, Peter, but seventy times seven!" (see Matthew 18:22).

If you are quick at arithmetic, you will have realized by now that 490 is considerably more than Simon's suggestion of seven. But in reality, Jesus was not proposing that Simon, or anybody else for that matter, should keep a long list of the number of times someone had been forgiven. He was not implying that when people chalked up 490 instances of forgiveness in the record books that they were free to do what they liked.

The Jewish colloquial phrase "seventy times seven" actually means a number so big that you do not even think about starting to count. In His reply to Peter's question, therefore, Jesus put no actual limit on the number of times Peter had to be willing to forgive.

The shocking truth is that if there is a limit on the number of times we are willing to forgive others, there will also have to be a limit on the number of times God is able to forgive us—the consequences of which none of us would ever wish to contemplate.

Remember what Jesus said in the Lord's Prayer: "Forgive us our debts, as we also have forgiven our debtors" (Matthew 6:12). In this extraordinary prayer, Jesus first introduced the idea that our being able to be forgiven could be related to our willingness to forgive others.

Since none of us would ever want there to be a limit on God's willingness to forgive us, there cannot be a limit on the number of times we must be willing to forgive others—no matter what they have done.

This might be easier for us to understand and accept if we remember that forgiveness has nothing to do with whether or not someone deserves to be forgiven—it is an act of love, not of justice.

## Broken Trust

Forgiveness does not have anything to do with future trust. A forgiven person may still be an untrustworthy person.

Sadly, many people have made the mistake of thinking that not only do they have to forgive but that their forgiveness also requires them to continue to trust that person as if nothing had happened. This is not the case, and in some cases this belief can be very dangerous.

I knew of a man who had sexually abused a friend's children while he babysat them. When the parents discovered what he had been doing, he seemed deeply repentant. He was full of remorse and heartbreak at what he had done. Initially he was suspended from his job in the church, but then he was forgiven by both the church leaders and the children's parents.

As part of the forgiveness process, he was given back his job as a teacher in the Sunday school. It was not long before it was discovered that he was abusing more children. It had been a terrible mistake to put him back in his old job where he faced such temptation and had easy access to children. He should not have been trusted in this way.

When a person has sinned against another human being, he or she has broken trust with both man and God. The offer of forgiveness does not always mean that trust has been restored. In most cases, trust has to be earned. It is never wise to put a person back in a position where an obvious weakness could possibly lead to further abuse.

## Complete Forgiveness

When you read the account of Peter's question and Jesus' answer in Matthew 18, it is often assumed that the reason that ongoing forgiveness is needed is because the offender keeps doing the same thing. In my experience, however, there is another more commonly encountered situation that requires repeated forgiveness.

When a person has been traumatized severely by the events in his or her life, there may be many levels of pain locked away in his or her memories. The first time a person forgives, therefore, is often an act of the will. This action can be contrary to the real, deeply buried feelings he or she may have. As feelings begin to surface—like waves on the seashore, seemingly without end—each memory becomes another opportunity to forgive. The waves will subside slowly, but he or she may need to forgive in excess of 490 times before the last amount of pain has been dissipated and forgiveness is complete.

## Complete Freedom

*How often do I have to forgive?* Until there is no longer any need to forgive and all the pain has been dealt with. At that point you have, with God's help, won a major victory in your life.

No longer will the chains of bondage from the past be able to hold you. You will be free once again to become the person God intended. For the rest of your life, you will be able to fulfill the destiny that God has reserved for you.

Jesus was concerned about the effect unforgiveness would have on His disciples, including you and me. If He had put a limit on the number of times we had to forgive, there would also be a limit on the freedom that we would experience through forgiving others.

Consider Pauline's experience with forgiveness. She had to forgive many times before she was able to be free of the brutal sexual abuse that was done to her as a child. For twenty years, Pauline slept on the floor under her bed. She had been too frightened to sleep on her bed because of what might happen to her. She felt safer under the bed.

She took an enormous step of courageous faith when she made that first faltering move toward forgiving those responsible. It was a step that saved her life. As the memories surfaced, she had to forgive time and time again. But every time she forgave, it was as if God were removing another layer of graveclothes from her personality.

Pauline is alive today because she learned Simon Peter's lesson—there can be no limit to forgiveness. She prayed the most powerful prayer on earth, "Father, forgive them." It was the miracle key she had been looking for, not only to overcome all of the inner anger at what others had done but also to know the love of Jesus in quite an extraordinary way.

Few people will suffer such awful things as Pauline did. Today you can know for certain that what God did for Pauline, He can do for you.

# What about God?

## The Need to Tell God We Are Sorry for Blaming Him

Deborah winced with pain as she tried to knock the stuffing out of a cushion with her fist.

"Surely if God really is God, He could have stopped all the bad things that have happened to me." Her anger was surfacing as she expressed her feelings to her counselor, and God was the target.

Deborah asked a very valid question.

"If God is as loving and all-powerful as Christians say He is, then why does He sit in heaven simply watching all sorts of terrible things happen on earth but doing nothing about them? It does not make sense. I'm not sure I want to know a God like that."

There was nothing wrong with her logic, and her feelings were understandable. But she was missing a few facts in the argument that led to a major distortion in her thinking and understanding.

## Free Will

The first fact that Deborah did not understand is that we are made in the image and likeness of God. Among other important things, this means that we, like God, have a free will. We were made with the capacity to make choices of our own.

Without free will, our lives would be reduced to the level of robots. We would have no capacity to choose what relationships we enter into. The joy of choice is key to personal enjoyment and pleasure.

Every human being is unique. We enjoy different things. Some people prefer pizza to hamburgers. Others love chicken. For vacations some people like to be by the sea while others prefer the mountains. Some love talking about politics while others prefer to play active sports. Variety and choice are central to our way of life.

No matter what our preferences may be, we have the freedom to choose what we like. Take away free will, and life as we know it ceases to exist. But having free will without the recognition of safe boundaries can be very dangerous.

## Safe Boundaries

Humankind's original sin was misusing free will and choosing to go outside of the boundaries set by God. It landed us in a huge mess. We chose to question what God said and to rebel against Him. The rest, as they say, is history.

In what is referred to as the Fall, we put ourselves willingly under an ungodly authority. That ungodly authority has done everything possible to destroy the relationship between God and humankind by encouraging one generation after another to dispense with godly order and go beyond the limits of God's boundaries.

We have seen that process happen in our own generation. The scriptural standards of morality, for example, which have formed the backbone of law and order in most Western nations for hundreds of years, have now virtually all been swept away by a rising tide of immorality, amorality and sexual promiscuity.

When young children go outside of the safe boundaries that their parents provide, they get into danger quickly. For this reason, parents provide the safety of a playpen. And if people could go where and how they liked on the roads, there would be innumerable accidents; therefore, our authorities provide rules and boundaries for traffic so that people can drive to places safely without the risk of head-on collisions.

Every year people in Canada go out on frozen lakes to enjoy themselves. Among other things, a frozen lake provides a wonderful facility for the thrill of traveling at high speeds across the ice on a snowmobile—provided, that is, people stay within the areas where the ice is known to be sufficiently thick for safety.

But every year there are some people who think they know better than the authorities, and they go beyond the recommended boundaries. In the process, some lose their lives. Every year there are families who are forced to mourn the loss of adventuresome or foolhardy explorers who went beyond the boundaries because they thought they knew best.

It is a bit like that with God's boundaries. The rebellion and independence within us make us want to live beyond the safety of the rules and boundaries provided by a loving and caring God. People have, for example, failed to understand that the Ten Commandments were not given by God to stop people from enjoying themselves, but rather to provide safe boundaries within which they can exercise free will without getting into danger.

## Evil and the Evil One

The Bible calls going beyond these boundaries trespassing or sinning. The consequence of using our free will to make sinful choices is that evil is given the opportunity to increase its influence in our lives.

In the Lord's Prayer, Jesus encourages us to pray, "Deliver us from evil" (Matthew 6:13 NASB) or, more accurately, "Deliver us from the evil one." There is an evil "god of this world" (2 Corinthians 4:4 NASB) who opposes every good thing that God prepared for His children.

When we pray this portion of the Lord's Prayer, we are asking God to help us make right choices so that we will be kept safely within God's boundaries. We are also praying for protection from the evil one who, from the beginning, has used his free will in the spiritual realms to tempt man to do wrong things and to oppose God. The Bible calls him Satan (see Matthew 4:10).

## Our Blameless God

In reality, then, all of the bad things that happen in this world are not God's fault. They are the consequences of the influence of the evil one and the wrong choices that people make as a result of his influence. We should not blame God for things that He is not responsible for.

If God were to use His ultimate power and authority to put a stop to everything that He does not like, He would have to take away our free will and put a stop to most of what is going on in the world. We would no longer be human beings capable of free will relationships with each other. We would no longer have the capacity to choose to enjoy a free will relationship with God.

The Bible tells us that Father God loved us so much that He sent His Son, Jesus, to show us how much He loves us. He wants to have a restored relationship with His children (see John 3:16–17).

We live in a fallen and evil world. We only have to read one newspaper or listen to one news bulletin to realize what a mess humankind has made of this world that God created.

Instead of blaming God for what humankind and the evil one has done, we should say to Him that we are sorry for blaming Him for things that were not His fault. This is an important step toward healing from the curse of bitterness that comes as a by-product of unforgiveness.

Saying we are sorry to God is another vital key to healing. If you use this key, it will remove a major obstacle that may be keeping you from being able to forgive others and from being able to pray the most powerful prayer on earth.

# 10 The Eight Steps to Freedom

## Instructions for Using God's Miracle Key

Your future is in your hands and God's hands. No matter how much the first part of your life has been damaged, you and God together can change your destiny so that in the second part of your life you will be free to become the person God intended you to be. You can know the blessing of God in a new way. The rest of your life begins today.

King David wrote of the wonderful blessings that God promises to those who understand and who choose gladly to walk within the boundaries that He has set. Here is what David wrote:

> The law of the LORD is perfect, *refreshing the soul.*
> The statutes of the LORD are trustworthy, *making*
> *wise the simple.*

> The precepts of the LORD are right, *giving joy to the
> heart.*
> The commands of the LORD are radiant, *giving
> light to the eyes.*
> The fear of the LORD is pure, *enduring forever.*
> The decrees of the LORD are *firm, and all of them
> are righteous.*
> They are *more precious than gold*, than much pure
> gold;
> they are *sweeter than honey*, than honey from the
> honeycomb.
> By them is your servant warned; *in keeping them
> there is great reward.*
>
> Psalm 19:7–11, emphasis added

In His Word, God has given wonderful guidelines for
living. He has also shown where the dangers are. In this
amazing psalm, God promises that if you choose to live
within the boundaries He has set (the law of the Lord),
He will revive your soul, give you His wisdom, give joy
to your heart, put light in your eyes, warn you of danger and enable you to enjoy His reward. What wonderful
promises.

When I look into the eyes of the hurting people who
come to me for help, I see the opposite of all of these wonderful blessings that God promises to those who follow
Him. I see hurt, disappointment, pain, anger, resentment,

bitterness and many other negative responses to the experiences of life.

One of the most important laws that God has shown us in His Word is the law of sowing and reaping. Paul tells us that we cannot ignore God's counsel and expect there not to be consequences. Paul says it this way: "God cannot be mocked. A man reaps what he sows" (Galatians 6:7).

This means that whatever sort of seed we sow in our lives, it will produce a harvest in keeping with the nature of the seed. In the context of this book, it means that if we sow unforgiveness, we will reap bitterness. And if we continue to sow the same seed throughout our days, bitterness will give rise to many harmful consequences. We will see these consequences both in our own life and in the lives of those with whom we interact daily. These consequences could even include physical symptoms and conditions.

"What must I do," I hear you saying, "if I don't want to grow this kind of crop in my life?"

If you have recognized your own need for forgiveness, decided to believe in Jesus and entrusted your life to Him, you have already taken huge steps forward. You are already at a new place in God. From this place you can pray the most powerful prayer on earth and begin to know God's healing.

Now is the time to get practical and understand the steps you need to take in order to apply this wonderful teaching from Scripture.

## Step 1: Make a Decision

We have already discussed that God has given to each one of us free will—the capacity to make choices.

The first step you need to take is to look back at every difficult situation that you have experienced and make a choice to forgive everyone who was involved. Only you can make this decision. No one else can do it for you.

I was asked to pray for a woman named Jane. Many years prior, Jane had been riding on the back of a two-man snowmobile on a frozen lake. Paul, the driver, lost control, and the machine somersaulted many times on the ice. Jane was thrown around like a rag doll as her body flew across the ice. Her head hit the ironhard surface repeatedly.

From that time on, Jane suffered major physical problems that affected her spine, her joints and her shoulders. She had years of medical and chiropractic treatment, but it did not give her permanent relief.

As I began to pray for Jane's physical problems, I was prompted to ask, "Have you forgiven Paul?" It was obvious from the look on her face that she had not forgiven the man who had caused her years of pain.

Jane had some serious work to do with God, so I told her that I could not pray for her until she had overcome this important obstacle. Some time passed before she was able to come to the place of choosing to forgive Paul and release him into the freedom of her forgiveness.

It had to be her choice. No amount of praying for her condition at that stage would have helped her. If I had started to pray for her physical problems while unforgiveness was creating a barrier to the love and power of God, nothing would have happened. She might have gone away thinking that God did not love her or that He could or would not heal her condition.

When I was able to pray for her again, the power of God was present to heal. Two decades of pain and spinal distortion were eliminated in a matter of minutes. The following day she was radiant, having gone for a run early in the morning and having done exercises that would previously have been impossible. She was a totally different person.

Jane's physical healing came down to whether or not she was willing to make a choice to forgive. Until she made that choice, God could do nothing.

Now it is your turn. Think about it. Are you willing to make the same choice Jane made and forgive every single person who has ever stolen something from you, abused you, betrayed you, talked ill of you or hurt you in any other way—regardless of the cost or the consequences?

Making this choice is your first step toward being able to pray the most powerful prayer on earth and to begin to reap a new crop of blessings in your life.

## Step 2: Make a List

Before you get to work, pray a short prayer. You can use your own words or say something like this:

*Thank You, Jesus, for teaching me the importance of forgiving others. Please help me to remember all the people who have hurt me so that I can forgive them from my heart.*

Prayers like this one do not have to be long or terribly formal. God is interested in you as a person and in the decisions of your heart, not in whether or not you are good with words.

If you have made the choice to forgive, it is time to get out a piece of paper and start making a list. One way of making your list is to think through your life. You can begin at the beginning and work forward, or you can start from where you are and work backward—it does not matter which direction you choose.

Whichever direction you decide to go, the two names that need to be at the top of your list are your parents—even if you think they were perfect. In reality, no parents are ever perfect, even though most parents do their very best within their personal and financial limitations. Think about what generational problems your parents may have carried to you from their parents and grandparents. (You may also need to repent of any ungodly reactions you had to things your parents did, as there are two sides to every relationship.)

Some parents, for example, can make it obvious in various ways that they would have preferred one of their children to have been the opposite gender than they were. Sometimes one child is cleverer than the others and is favored for this or other reasons. There are many issues for which you need to dig deep in your spirit to make a godly choice to forgive.

Such things as abuse, victimization or cruelty are obvious, but the less obvious ones must not be overlooked. When you start on a journey of forgiveness, ask the Lord to direct your thinking so that you cover all of the ground. You may need to do this on several occasions as further things come to mind.

When you have spent ample time allowing God to lead you through the memories of your family and you have forgiven every negative experience that your parents passed on to you, then ask God to remind you of things that have happened with others. Be careful and systematic. Give God a chance to remind you of people you might have forgotten.

Think about your friends, classmates or any other people with whom you have shared something of your life. Think back on every year of your life and everywhere you have been—school, work, church, sporting events, vacations and so on. Think through things like being physically or emotionally abused, being abandoned, laughed at or bullied, being told that you are stupid, no good or useless, or being made to feel ugly, worthless or inferior. Children and adults can take to heart many hurtful things and store them up on the inside.

Every time you think of someone you need to forgive, write down his or her name and the reason you need to forgive that person. Do not rush this process. Give yourself plenty of space and time.

Some names will cause you more pain than others. You might even have difficulty writing down some of the names. You might think that you do not want to forgive a specific person, or you might convince yourself that they do not deserve to be forgiven. If you have difficulties like this, look back to the specific chapter in this book that deals with the particular problem you are having, read it again and determine to press on. Remember, you have made a decision to forgive, so ask God to help you.

And do not forget to put your own name on the list. If you have ever cursed yourself by saying something like "I'll never forgive myself," you are probably struggling with the consequences of those words. You need to take some time to forgive yourself for your own mistakes.

## Step 3: Start to Forgive

Now is the time for another short prayer. Pray something like this:

*Lord Jesus, thank You for dying on the cross that I might be forgiven. I am sorry for my own sins, and I ask*

*You to be my Savior and the Lord of my life. And now
please forgive me for the things that I have done wrong.
Please help me to forgive all of the people on my list.*

As you go down your list, pray carefully over each name.
Remind yourself what it was that they did to you, and then
pray something like this:

*I now choose to forgive* [name] *for* [brief description
of what was done to you], *and I release* [name] *into
the freedom of my forgiveness. I will not hold these
things against* [name] *anymore.*

As you pray through your list, you will find that God is
changing you slowly from the inside out. You will be leaving behind all the bad things that resentment and bitterness
have brought into your life, and you will begin to emerge
like a butterfly at the beginning of a new era.

## Step 4: Ask God to Set You Free

You can do this after each prayer of forgiveness, or you
can say it at the end after you have prayed through your
list. Whichever way you choose, pray something like this:

*Thank You, Lord, for helping me forgive* [name]. *I ask
now that You would set me free from every ungodly*

*influence that* [name] *has had on my life. Please cut the ropes that have held me tightly to the pain of the past.*

## Step 5: Say You Are Sorry for Blaming God

If at various times of your life you have blamed God for things that you now know were not His responsibility, you will want to tell Him you are sorry and ask Him to forgive you. You can use words like these:

*I am sorry, God, for blaming You for the bad things that have happened in my life. I now know You did not want these things to happen. Please forgive me.*

## Step 6: Pray the Most Powerful Prayer on Earth

Praying the most powerful prayer on earth is what this book is all about! We have had to travel quite a journey through your life to get to this point. When Jesus prayed, "Father, forgive them, for they do not know what they are doing" (Luke 23:34), there was no sin, unforgiveness, resentment, bitterness or ungodly anger in His heart. Jesus was free to be able to pray this most amazing prayer with a pure heart even in the midst of His own pain. I wonder what thoughts the Roman soldiers had as they nailed Him to the cross and heard His prayer?

I said earlier that forgiveness is an act of love, not of justice. The heart of Jesus toward His accusers and killers was a heart of love. Above all else, He wanted everyone to be able to come to know God and to experience God's forgiveness for themselves.

Before Jesus' execution, His disciples must have wondered what He really meant when He taught them, "Love your enemies, do good to those who hate you, bless those who curse you, pray for those who mistreat you" (Luke 6:27–28). Now they knew. Jesus put His own teaching into practice as He prayed, "Father, forgive them."

Jesus died with these words on His lips and in His heart. He had given no ground to His accusers. As a result, neither the evil one nor any of the powers of darkness could touch Him. This was the most powerful prayer on earth because it led to the resurrection morning.

### Step 7: Pray that Jesus Will Forgive Them

The final stage in offering forgiveness to others is to pray as Jesus did. Pray that those who have hurt you will be forgiven for everything they have done. Of course, you cannot pray such a prayer with an honest heart until you have first forgiven people for what they have done to you. When you forgive, God will release healing into the consequences of your past and will work miracles that will transform every area of your life.

To pray as Jesus did is to make a choice to bless selflessly the lives of others—yes, even those who have hurt you. By doing so, you are following the example of Jesus and are helping other people have the opportunity to know God for themselves. This is the greatest blessing we can bestow on others.

Those you have forgiven still have free will regarding how they will respond to what God does in their lives as a result of your prayer. You are not responsible for any choices they make.

―――――――――――

Corrie ten Boom became famous for her and her family's work in preserving the lives of over 800 Jews who were being pursued by the Nazis during World War II. Four members of her family lost their lives because of their commitment.

Corrie and her sister, Betsy, both spent time in the Ravensbruck death camp. While Corrie survived the death camp, Betsy died just before the end of the war. When Corrie came home, she realized that her life was a gift from God and that she needed to share what she and Betsy had learned. Instead of telling of the horrors of the camp and how awful her captors had been, she felt compelled to share what God had taught her. "There is no pit so deep that God's love is not deeper still."[1]

1. Corrie ten Boom and Elizabeth Sherrill, *The Hiding Place* (Minneapolis: Chosen Books, 2006), 11.

Corrie had learned to use God's miracle key in one of earth's darkest places. Because of this, at the age of 53 she began a worldwide ministry and entered into an era of great blessing. This ministry took her into more than 60 countries over the next 32 years. There was nothing from Corrie's past that could hold her in chains of bondage. God's miracle key had set her free!

———————————

The family of Stephen Oake also learned to pray the most powerful prayer on earth. Stephen was an outstanding Christian police officer who served the Greater Manchester Police. In January 2003, he was killed tragically in the line of duty when a suspect stabbed him. Stephen left behind grieving parents, a heartbroken wife and young children.

Stephen's father, a retired senior police officer, and Stephen's wife were quick to declare to the press and reporters that they had forgiven the man who had robbed their family of a son, husband and father.[2]

This was a very high-profile incident in the United Kingdom. The nation was stunned, not only by the tragedy itself, but also by the family's genuinely Christlike reaction to what had happened. The fruit of this remarkable response has been that the family has been freed from the chains of

2. Robin Oake, *Father, Forgive: How to Forgive the Unforgivable* (Bletchley, UK: Authentic Media Limited, 2007).

bitterness. Their ability to forgive has also provided some very significant opportunities for the Gospel to be shared—especially among the police officers.

Not only does God's miracle key have an effect on those you have prayed for, but it also opens the door for God to pour His blessings on your life in a new way. No longer will you be chained to the past by anyone who has hurt you. You are free!

Even when it seems impossible, you will be able to forgive with God's help. Ask Jesus to give you His love for all those who have hurt you. Pray "Father, forgive them." Let it become the most powerful prayer on earth for you as well.

## Step 8: Expect Your Resurrection Morning

When Jesus rose from the dead and burst out of the tomb, He was no longer wearing the graveclothes in which His body had been wrapped. As you break out from the chains of your past by genuinely forgiving the people on your list, you will experience a transformation like a resurrection morning.

Jesus promised to make all things new (see 2 Corinthians 5:17; Revelation 21:5). The graveclothes of bitterness will be gone, and God's divine law of blessing will start to operate in your life.

# 11 It Is Up to You
## Final Thoughts

Your life is unique. All that has happened to you since the moment you were conceived is your personal story. It will remain your own story—yours and yours alone—until the day you die and leave this world behind. The same is true for the rest of your life. What happens to you between now and when you die matters more to you than to anyone else in the world.

Your life has only two parts: the part you have already lived and the part yet to be lived. The first part is always getting longer, and the second is always getting shorter.

All of us want to enjoy and make the most of whatever time we have left to live on this planet. What you do now could be the difference between being blessed abundantly for the rest of your life or struggling to keep your head above water in a sea of disappointment, resentment, bitterness, anger, hatred or revenge.

The sooner you really understand that there is a direct connection between how you respond to the difficult moments of the first part of your life and how much you are able to enjoy and be fulfilled in the second part of your life, the sooner you will be able to start living life again to the fullest extent. When the ropes of unforgiveness are truly cut, there is nothing that can keep you bound to the pain of your past.

No good whatsoever comes from hanging on to memories of bitterness, no matter what others may have done. The longer you hang on to them, the more the second part of your life is eaten into by the first. Remaining in unforgiveness gives the past a right to haunt you in the present.

The Bible is full of promises of restoration and hope for the people of God; however, there are always conditions attached to them. One of those conditions is choosing to forgive. What is stopping you? You have absolutely nothing to lose and everything to gain!

# 12 Personal Stories of Healing through Forgiveness

For more than twenty years, I have been teaching about forgiveness and ministering to people who have come to our centers for help. In the early days, I discovered that forgiveness is perhaps the most important element in anyone's pilgrimage toward wholeness. That was certainly what Jesus must have thought. He spoke out strongly about the consequences of not forgiving others. "But if you do not forgive others their sins, your Father will not forgive your sins" (Matthew 6:15).

Those years of ministry are like a long corridor of time for me. The corridor has framed pictures on its walls that display the people whom God touched deeply on a healing retreat, during a training course, at a conference or in a personal ministry appointment.

I can see many of them now in my mind as I write these words—people who I will never forget because of what God did in their lives. I want to allow some of those faces to come off the wall and share for themselves something of what God did as they turned the forgiveness master key and discovered that the Master Himself was right there, ready to bring His wonderful healing into the depths of their lives.

Some suffered great rejection by their parents. Others were abused sexually. Yet others were injured in accidents that were not their fault. Some were betrayed or robbed. Sadly, some of these problems were caused by people they thought they could trust—even fellow Christians or members of their own families. The catalog of possible pain in the lives of human beings is longer than most people's capacity to imagine.

To some people it seems as though their lives have been destroyed by what has happened, and there is little hope for their future. And yet for all of these people, there is one key they can turn that will begin the process of healing from the past. It can transform both their present and their future. They have to turn God's master key and forgive those who have hurt them.

## Frida's Story

On occasion, a story reveals a past that has been so horrendous that it makes you wonder if it would ever be possible for a human being to forgive. I will never forget a young woman from Rwanda who introduced herself at the beginning of one of our training schools at Ellel Grange.[1]

She radiated the beauty of Jesus, but she also bore the scars of the Rwandan genocide that occurred in 1994. In this genocide, a million Tutsi people were killed by Hutus in a tribal war that lasted one hundred days. Frida was the only surviving member of her immediate family. One day, all of her fifteen close relatives, including grandparents, parents, brothers and sisters, were gathered together and asked how they wanted to die. If you were wealthy enough to buy your own bullet, you could be shot and get it over with quickly, but if you were poor, it was not that easy.

Frida's family was poor. Her mother chose the machete, and Frida chose to be hit over the back of the head with a blunt instrument. She thought that would be quick. One by one all her family were executed and pushed into a shallow grave, including Frida. But Frida did not actually die. She was buried alive and covered. Fourteen hours later, someone heard a sound from the grave and dug her out.

Later, when the genocide was all over, she became a Christian and started to read the Bible. It was in the Bible

---

1. Ellel Grange is the headquarters of Ellel Ministries International where this work of healing began in 1986.

that she read about forgiveness, and she knew that she had to go to the jail to forgive the man who had killed her family. That act freed her from the consequences of bitterness and any possibility of a desire for revenge. Without forgiveness, she would have experienced a lifetime of bondage to the people who had done those terrible things.

At one of our conferences, she told her story and declared that she forgave everyone who had been involved in those terrible events. Before her courageous act of forgiveness, she had been suffering awful nightmares and constant pain in the place where she had been hit. That night God healed her completely. She was freed from the pain and from the recurring nightmares. Her full remarkable story is told in her book *Chosen to Die, Destined to Live* that is published by Sovereign World.

Today she is married to a pastor in Kigali, the capital city of Rwanda. She and her husband minister hope and healing to their people. Frida not only found healing for herself when she turned God's master key, but she has been able to share her story to many hundreds, if not thousands, of people who experienced something similar to what she did. Each of them can join in the experience of being blessed through the process of forgiveness.

When people tell me that the events in their particular story are too hard to forgive, I tell them Frida's story. Frida chose to forgive, regardless of how impossible that seemed, and she experienced healing as a result.

## John's Story

John's story was different, but he still had to begin at the same place—forgiving those who had hurt him.

> God has transformed my life. I came from a background of rejection, fear, pain, violence, hate, drug addiction, homosexuality, prostitution, occultism and depression. When I met the Holy Spirit, my life changed completely. God has used Ellel Ministries to help me see deeper into my life, and that has brought true healing and deliverance.
>
> Now I have my life back. I finally feel like I am living again. The love of God has changed me, and I am free. I have found the purpose for which I am here.

## Simon's Story

Simon described how he used the master key of forgiveness to enter into an arena of life that would have been impossible for him previously.

> Walking down the road of forgiveness has been a key to unlocking the treasures of heaven in my life. It is a key that opens the gates of heaven for God's blessings to be poured out. He is so faithful.
>
> I have learned that forgiving someone is not about taking away the responsibility of the person who hurt me. It does

not mean that the violation was somehow okay. It is about releasing it all into the hands of God and letting Him be the judge of everything. As challenging and painful as this road undeniably is, His mercy and gentleness are far greater.

A step of obedience is always followed by the healing touch of the Holy Spirit that is so sweet and tender yet so fair and just. I am allowed to see my own weaknesses and what my sins have caused others. I know He carried my guilt on the cross as well. Glory be to God for the cross of Jesus!

I pray that there will always be those who choose to travel on this road. It is the road of the Kingdom of God where the Prince of Peace rules. No powers of darkness can prevail against Him. He truly brought me out into open landscapes where I can lie down and rest. Be assured, He does redeem the years that the locust has eaten. His thoughts and plans for me are always for good and not for evil.

## Linda's Story

Many of those who face the deepest pain have been abused sexually. When the abuse has been perpetrated by the victim's own father, it is especially unbearable. When a father violates that position of trust, he causes damage that can take half a lifetime to face. Sadly, many of those who suffered the most never find the answer that only Jesus can provide.

Linda was one of those whose life was in the balance when she came to Ellel for help. She had experienced years of medical intervention for her brokenness, but there was nothing more the doctors could do. When you hear her story, you will be able to rejoice at the miracle-working power of God that was released in her life through forgiveness. She turned the master key, and as a result, she saw God rescue her from the miry clay and put her feet on a rock.

My father abused me sexually throughout my childhood. Although my mother knew what was happening, she did not try to protect me. In fact, she was angry at me and the situation. As a result, she withheld her love from me. I took all the blame on myself and grew up full of guilt and self-hatred. I became depressed and suicidal and eventually ended up in a psychiatric hospital.

Mercifully, God had a rescue plan for my life. This plan began to unfold when I was given the opportunity to receive Christian counseling and ministry. I learned that a big key to healing was forgiveness, and I realized I needed to forgive my parents for the cruelty that they had rained on me. Forgiving them was not something I really struggled with. Jesus had given the instruction in the Bible, so I obeyed.

But I didn't experience any great sense of release. I was still so afraid of people that I wouldn't go outside, and I hid when anyone came to the house. I still hated myself intensely and battled with suicidal thoughts and the desire to self-harm.

Gradually I began to understand that my forgiveness was incomplete if it didn't involve more than a mental decision that was detached from pain. I realized I had to feel the emotional responses that the cruelty of my childhood evoked. I had to face the pain, anger and strong sense of injustice that I had buried deep down inside myself. And in the midst of feeling the intensity of these emotions, I had to face the issue of forgiveness all over again.

My self-hatred was a defense. Believing I was bad covered the fact that it was my parents' actions toward me that were bad and that I had not deserved to be abused.

I repented of hating myself, and gradually the Lord helped me to connect with my hidden emotions and to embrace the truth of how I really felt. There wasn't just pain and anger, but desperate cries of "It's not fair!" and "I wanted it to be different!" There was bitterness, resentment, a desire for revenge and jealousy of what others had that I didn't have. The whole process was like having a dirty dressing taken off a deep, festering wound.

I couldn't have faced it on my own. This was a work of the Holy Spirit. He asked me not only to face the truth in my innermost parts as He enabled me, but also to allow Him into the wound. My job was to take my pain to the foot of the cross, and I was to choose to forgive even in the midst of feeling my bitterness and unforgiveness.

This was hard, and it took time. On the one hand, I battled with the injustice and pain of being abused, the emptiness of feeling unloved and my stubborn resistance to forgiveness, and on the other hand, the conviction from Jesus that I needed to forgive. Jesus, who was wholly sinless, had cried out, "Father, forgive them," when He was nailed to the cross.

It was important for me to be brutally honest with God while I was battling my bitterness and unforgiveness. I had to own that this was me. This was how I felt, and I couldn't change that. It was only then that I could receive His enabling to do what was impossible for me.

I wanted to obey Him. I had previously made a choice in my head to forgive, but it was Jesus who enabled me to forgive in my heart. Gradually, I learned to take the pain and negative emotions to Him each time I felt them, and little by little He enabled me to forgive. I was able to receive His comfort where I needed it. What a gracious God He is!

I can say truthfully that my life is completely different today. I have an inner security and strength that come from having allowed God into my deepest place of pain. I no longer suffer with the fears that were once debilitating. I am free of all psychiatric medication, I have been signed off a lifetime-incapacity benefit, I am in paid employment and I am free to fully enter into life with my family and friends in a way that I never thought could be possible. I am so thankful and give Him all the praise, all the glory and all the honor.

## Johann's Story

Johann is typical of many people who get into bad and dangerous habits without understanding the reasons why. They do not understand how things that happened to them in their past can be at the root of today's problems. This is how Johann told his story:

I have been a sort-of Christian for about ten years, but a re-born Christian for only a year. I am praising Jesus so much for everything He has done. He has led me into a deeper relationship with Him than I could ever have imagined.

I had gotten involved with the wrong group of friends and started using drugs. I used cocaine for over two years. During that time, I got offered a new job. I worked on the fifth floor next to a woman named Lucy.

After I had been working for a week, she asked me a simple question, "Are you a Christian?"

When I told her that I was, she gave me a teaching series from Peter Horrobin called "Ministering Hope." I didn't listen to the CDs—I thought they'd be too boring. But a few days later, I had an accident that forced me to travel by car. For some reason, the CDs had been left in my car.

I started listening to them. It was like God talking into my spirit. I got born again in my car on the way to work! I realized it was time to move back into the hands of God. I managed to quit the drugs without even going to rehab just by listening to Peter's teaching.

God showed me how to get healed on the inside by forgiving the man who had molested me at a young age—which I now knew was the cause of my unhappiness. God showed me how important it was to get healed at the root of the problem where the unhappiness started. My life changed so much.

But after a few months, I was in another accident. I learned there had been a doctor driving a car that was a few cars behind me. He saw the accident happen and prevented my ribs from puncturing my lungs. People told me that I was the most fortunate person in the world.

Doctors told me that there was a chance that I would lose one of my legs, but I kept my faith in God. Now I have recovered fully from the accident without losing my leg. God is so powerful!

I could not understand why God allowed this accident because I loved Him so much and tried my best to keep in line with Him. The answer was very simple. God will take the bad things that happen to you and change them into good things. I just want to praise and thank Him for helping me through this accident.

Last but not least, I was baptized. I thank Jesus again for this special gift in my life. God used Peter's teaching to give me a second chance to experience His love and faithfulness that will never ever fail.

When Johann got into drugs, he was in a downward spiral that had begun with childhood molestation. Children often do not know how to cope with the consequences of what happens to them, and they usually bury the pain and hurt. But pain such as this is buried alive. Unless it is healed by Jesus, it will have self-destructive consequences. Taking drugs is just one of the many coping mechanisms that people can use.

Fortunately, Johann got to the root of the problem quickly after he was born again. He forgave his molester and asked God to cut him free from this ungodly relationship. Johann turned the master key and now lives to serve his Lord.

## Forgiveness and Healing in Africa

The Ellel Ministries team has conducted training conferences in Africa. Teachings on forgiveness are always a vital part of the foundational instruction at such events. This is how the leader of the mission reported about a particular event.

A woman gave a powerful testimony of the freedom she experienced after forgiving her son-in-law's family. They had persecuted her and her husband physically and emotionally after their daughter died during the birth of their grandchild. The forgiveness teaching was so critical to them.

There were many others who also needed to forgive. So many difficult things had happened in so many people's lives. Many were crying as they forgave. I realized yet again how important teaching about forgiveness is in Africa, as so many people here have experienced rejection.

God did an amazing restoration in the life of one particular man. He told a testimony about the release that he was experiencing after he forgave the people who had killed his son. After the conference closed, he brought his five-year-old daughter for prayer. Her little legs were very uneven. God did a miracle and healed this girl's legs to be completely even! We serve a God of miracles! We rejoiced at God's goodness!

## Forgiveness and Healing in Malaysia

One lady heard the teaching at a conference and put what she had learned into practice immediately with her family. She later wrote to tell us what happened.

> God impressed me to pray for inner healing for my mom as she had gone through a lot of rejection. She was given away as soon as she was born. Even today, she doesn't know who her real parents are. She was abused verbally and told she had brought bad luck to the family. At the age of sixteen she was forced to marry my father and was made to work, cook, clean and look after my father's entire family.
>
> I am so thankful to God for teaching me about inner healing. Because I was healed, I could help my mom. God healed and delivered her of all the pain she had been carrying for so many, many years. She will be eighty soon.
>
> I have led my mom to repentance and helped her to be born again. Jesus helped her to remember the people she needed to forgive. As she started to cry, the Holy Spirit just took over and brought deliverance and healing. God is so good!

## Elaine's Story

On healing retreats that are run by Ellel Ministries, the leaders provide very practical teaching on how to live the Christian life. They explain about how Jesus needs to be Lord of every area of our being, and a lot of space and time is dedicated to helping people forgive those who have hurt them.

Elaine's story is a wonderful account of how God can heal even the deepest pain. He can also restore our experience of life so that every area is totally transformed by the presence of God. A master key is a key that will open every lock. God's master key is that powerful.

I have been a Christian for over twenty years and have enjoyed a wonderful walk with my Savior; however, due to a series of events that happened over the last six years or so, that relationship was strained. I was hurting and struggling to come to terms with the traumatic events. Through this hurt, rejection, depression and confusion, I looked for love and acceptance in all the wrong places. My sinful life caused me to think I had lost my salvation.

My life became a constant struggle of trying to do the right things while also battling depression, loneliness, self-rejection and many other negative influences. As a Christian, I knew I should give it all to God. While I know that He is a fair and a just God and that everything works together for good, I felt so much shame, guilt and injustice that suicide was a constant companion. It seemed to offer a way out of the pain. Thankfully, by God's mercy, the attempts that I did make were unsuccessful. Looking back, I now realize that He really does have good plans for my life.

I came for a healing retreat expecting that God would do something, but never in my wildest dreams did I ever imagine He would do so much.

Through the excellent teaching and wonderful, sensitive counseling, the Holy Spirit revealed roots to my problems, and He helped me understand how these roots had given the enemy inroads into my life.

At the start of the retreat, I explained how my life seemed like a recipe that was all messed up. Through Lordship prayer, I was able to separate out the different ingredients of this recipe. Each ingredient was an area of my life. The Holy Spirit ministered to the areas that needed His touch. As they were dealt with, I was able to feel love like I had never known before.

For the first time ever, I knew my heavenly Father as my daddy. He loved me in a way I had never encountered before. I have known of His love for many years, and I have experienced His grace and mercy more times than I will ever know, but during this weekend Father God touched my heart. I realized that I do not have to strive, work, perform or jump through any hoops to earn His love and approval.

I was free to see Him the way He wants me to see Him. In light of this revelation, I walked around the grounds and the grass seemed greener. The trees were so exciting, and the chorus of birds at dawn was overwhelming. I walked down the sidewalk both laughing and crying. I had a great big smile from ear to ear. I was walking with my Daddy God, and I was free to enjoy His love. I did not need to say anything. It was like we were communicating through His creation, and I knew that He knew I was so happy.

Later, during worship as we sang "I have changed your name," I was so overwhelmed with His love that my tears flowed and flowed. It was lovely to cry from a heart that was beating once again because of God's love. I had often spoken out Scriptures about God's love for me, but that weekend the knowledge of His love dropped eighteen inches from my head and really became alive in my heart!

What an extraordinary testimony of the transforming love of God; however, without choosing to turn the master key, none of the joy that Elaine experienced could have been hers.

We pray for many people who have suffered the consequences of accidents. Sometimes pain and trauma have been stored up inside of them for many years. Often resentment and bitterness toward those who caused the accident are also stored up inside. This limits the healing process severely.

Jim was healed of asthma after forgiving his father for deliberately letting him be crushed against a concrete floor at a young age. Bill was healed of the fears and trauma that had gripped his life for forty years after not being protected by his mother as he pulled a saucepan of boiling water down onto his chest. The list of people and circumstances is endless.

Jennifer's story is a little different. In her situation, it was not other people that she needed to forgive. She had to use the master key to forgive herself.

## Jennifer's Story

I was in a tragic car accident many years ago that killed two family members. Since then I have suffered from severe back pain. To try and control the pain, I have had to take several strong painkillers every day.

As the Ellel Ministry team prayed with me, I discovered that I was feeling guilty about the accident. At the time of the accident, I had been looking after my brothers and sisters while my mom was partying. When the team asked me what part of the accident I felt responsible for, I thought, *How could I be responsible for anything? I was only a kid!*

They encouraged me to forgive myself. But to my shock and horror, I found myself saying that I couldn't forgive myself. In my heart, I believed I was responsible for the accident because I had insisted that my mom take us home. I had no problem forgiving others, but it took me time to get to a place where I could actually forgive myself.

I felt an immediate release in my physical body after they prayed over me. I had been so traumatized that something of me had been locked away on the inside. I was told this often happens in severe trauma. They prayed that the Lord would heal that broken part and fully heal and restore me on the inside.

Three things happened as a result. First, I have slept like a baby and have been pain free ever since. Before this time, I had been prayed for many times, but I had always woken up the next day back where I started—very sore and disappointed.

Second, and this is hard to put into words, my personality seems to have changed for the better. I'm more confident— especially at work. I used to feel quite immature, and it bothered me. Now I really feel good about myself.

Third, I am excited to say that I have not had to take the medication. I did not even have to wean myself off it gradually, and I am doing very well. I'm just in awe of how God works and how situations keep us in bondage. We can't get out of them by ourselves. God is truly amazing!

Jennifer's story is not unusual. Forgiveness is a master key to healing in the very deepest recesses of our minds. What is unusual in Jennifer's story is that the person she most needed to forgive was herself.

Another lady had struggled with chronic fatigue syndrome for seven years. Part of her healing included forgiving herself for the ungodly sexual relationships in which she had participated many years previously. She reported to us that nearly a month later, she was still full of the joy of the Lord. Her back problem was healed, her relationships with others were changing and lots of fears had gone. She was on a pilgrimage of healing, and every day or two she noticed something was different.

She summed it up this way: "After twenty-eight years of Christian struggle, the blockage between me and the Lord has been removed! I'm now enrolled in our church's prayer-ministry training course so I can learn how to help others experience this freedom, too."

## Jan's Story

Jan was another lady who discovered that forgiving herself was the most important thing she had to do. Turning the master key of forgiveness for herself proved to be the best thing she ever did.

I left home when I was a teenager, and I made a lot of bad choices. I was covered with the filth of shame. And then a few years ago, I gave my life to Christ. I raced right into ministry because I knew that Christ had redeemed and forgiven me. I knew that He had washed me clean. However, I never forgave myself. I couldn't do that, and I didn't know how.

I could say to people that I wanted them to experience God's grace, but I felt like I was a fake because I didn't own that for myself. I believed it, but I didn't give myself permission to receive it by forgiving myself. I hit this wall, and things got so hard.

The weekend of the retreat, the labels that I have worn for four decades were ripped off. I am not ashamed anymore, and I am so thankful for that. There was no room left on my rejection tree because I filled so much of it up! I want to encourage all of you that He can give you what it takes to forgive yourself so that you can live in freedom for Him.

## Michael's Story

Sometimes people come for prayer for one thing, but because God knows them better than they know themselves, they find that they have to face deeper issues. This was Michael's experience.

I arrived at the healing retreat expecting to deal with two traumatic accidents, but God had other ideas. I found myself having to deal with forgiveness in a mighty way! I also had to forgive myself for a lot of things, which was really liberating.

The Holy Spirit touched me deeply and filled me afresh. I am no longer in a spiritual wilderness. I had been so dry for the last few years that I had lost the joy of the Lord. For the first time in my life, I feel as though I am truly me.

I have never understood why I used to say, "I wish I could just be me," but now I know! I had to get rid of all the rubbish that was in my life before I could reclaim my true self—as God created me to be. I now know who I am. Praise the Lord!

## Connie's Story

Sometimes we find that people are damaged by circumstances that are beyond anyone's immediate control. There is nothing obvious that needs to be forgiven. But what I have seen in circumstances like this is that there is often a buried belief that somehow or other it must be God's fault.

Part of the prayer ministry in these situations has to include a prayer of repentance to God for blaming Him for things that are consequences of living in a fallen world. Satan is ultimately behind everything that is bad. Connie's story falls into this category of deep inner pain. She truly experienced a miracle of God's grace as the earliest issues in her life were dealt with.

> I went to a healing service not knowing what God needed to do, but I was open to Him. I went forward for prayer, and as a result of this ministry both of the cataracts in my eyes shrunk. I had been blind in my right eye for ten years, but after receiving prayer was able to see shapes with that eye. I was also able to hear in my right ear, which I had been unable to hear with for years. I also had prayer about the severe curvature of my spine, and this proved to be the start of the healing of my back condition.
>
> During the prayer ministry, I found myself crying like a baby. As the Holy Spirit moved upon me, spiritual chains broke off, and I sensed that something had left my body. With that release came deliverance, and I was set free from bondage.

I saw Jesus through a mist wearing a white robe. He came, put His arms around me and said, "It's over, no more tears, you are saved. You are My child, My princess, and I have a special place for you."

My life has been changed—completely turned around. I am walking daily with Him, experiencing the Holy Spirit strengthening me. He fills me with His joy and love, and He is continuing the healing in my body—my hips, head, eyes and ears. My confidence is back, and I can go out on my own. God has worked miracles and other people have seen the difference in me. I feel like my life has changed forever.

When praying for people like Connie, we always pray to forgive anyone in the generational line who has done anything that could possibly have resulted in negative inherited conditions. Sometimes that prayer alone begins a dramatic stage in the healing and restoration. Lamentations 5:7 tells us that "Our ancestors sinned and are no more, and we bear their punishment." We cannot deny the fact that children can suffer because of what their parents and grandparents have done. On many occasions, we have seen how God began a deep work of healing in people who were able to forgive those who had gone before.

## Olga's Story

Olga was brought up in Communist Russia. The parenting and ancestry she received left her very damaged emotionally, spiritually and even physically. The generational consequences of everything from occultism and witchcraft to the harshness of Russian communism had left its mark on Olga's life. This resulted in a twisted spine and constant pain in her back that required regular treatment. It was affecting her life in a dramatic way. She had never linked her physical problems with the spiritual roots, but when she heard the message about how to forgive, she knew immediately what she had to do. Here is her story of what happened:

> I was brought up in Communist Russia. I always felt that I was under a generational curse because of my father's sincere embrace of Communism. In addition to that, my grandmother was associated with occult practices and witchcraft in pre-Communist Russia. I didn't know that my severe and constant back pain was in any way connected to that. But once I learned about the possible impact of such things, I recognized immediately their relationship to my pain. At the conference, I prayed deeply for freedom from both generational sin and my mother's overcontrolling spirit. I forgave from the deepest parts of my being. As I did so, I felt a ripple effect going down and then up my spine. Each vertebra responded to the movement of the Holy Spirit!
>
> My back has been healed. Since then, the pain from my back has gone. Every vertebra feels free from the tension from the past. No more visits to the chiropractor. No more fear

of the past or shadows waiting to catch me in my moment of doubt—they are powerless! They are gone. Hallelujah!

## Bob's Story

Rejection comes in many forms. For Bob it was so deep that it went to the very center of his being. Even as a little boy, Bob's dad did not own that Bob was his. He felt that his son was an embarrassment, and he did everything he could to disown the child. Years later, Bob had to know what the truth really was. When it was confirmed who Bob's father was, a new phase of his life began as they tried to build a relationship. But the master key had not yet been turned in the lock of Bob's life. When it was, a miracle took place!

The most difficult issue in my life was the rejection that I felt from my earliest memories. I was the only son of a single mother. My father had, as a matter of legal strategy rather than real conviction, denied I was his son when I was very young. Even now, I remember the day when I took the blood test that confirmed his paternity. From that point on, I spent an enormous amount of energy trying to be a good son and trying to make him (whether he liked it or not) a good father.

While on a Healing Retreat at Ellel, I asked God to break the ungodly soul ties to my father. I was led to forgive him. The result was an immediate and dramatic positive change in his life. This change manifested itself at the very hour those ties were broken even though he was miles away! Suddenly, he was liberated to be the good dad that he wanted to be, and I was liberated to love him in a godly way while still building my relationship with my true Father in heaven. Now my children enjoy their grandfather when he visits in ways that I never enjoyed as a son. I love him with an unconditional love only Christ could have taught me to give. From Ellel's teaching, I learned that there is no healing without forgiveness, and there is no forgiveness without genuine, Christlike love. Like salvation itself, this is in fact a simple choice. Learn it for yourself and be amazed like I was at what God can do!

## In Conclusion

These stories are all real stories about real people. They are people like you and me who were struggling with the issues of life without realizing that the most important key to their problems was found in forgiveness.

The amazing prayer that Jesus prayed was truly the most powerful prayer on earth. You can start praying it now and begin to experience God's presence, love and power in your life in a new way.

The key is in your hand. It is a key of miracles that only you can use. Let this day be the beginning of a new era of blessing for you. Now is the time to act. I pray that as you think carefully about the contents of this book and as you resolve to use the miracle key, God will meet you at your point of need. I pray that you will experience the freedom of forgiveness and the transforming power of His love. I pray that you will be encouraged to ask God to help you turn this master key and see His miracle-working power in your life!

# ABOUT THE AUTHOR

**PETER HORROBIN** is the founder and international director of Ellel Ministries. Ellel Ministries was first established in 1986 as a ministry of healing in northwest England. Many lives were transformed through what God was doing, and the ministry could not be contained in one location. In the early nineties, the work quickly expanded to other parts of the country and into eastern Europe. Today the ministry is established in well over 50 operational centers in over 35 different countries.

Peter was born in 1943 in Bolton, Lancashire, and was brought up in Blackburn, also in northern England. His parents gave him a firm Christian foundation with a strong evangelical emphasis. His early grounding in the Scriptures would equip him for future ministry.

After graduating from Oxford University with a degree in chemistry, he spent a number of years lecturing in colleges and universities. He transitioned from the academic environment to the world of business, where he founded a series of successful publishing and bookselling companies.

In his twenties, Peter started to restore a vintage sports car (an Alvis Speed 20) but discovered that its chassis was bent. As he looked at the wreck of his broken car, wondering if it could ever be repaired, he sensed God saying, *You can restore this broken car, but I can restore broken lives. Which is more important?* It was obvious that broken lives were more important than broken cars, so the vision for restoring the lives of people was birthed in Peter's heart.

A few years later, he was asked to help a person who had been sexually abused. Through this experience, God further opened up to him the vision of a healing ministry. He prayed daily into this vision until 1986 when God brought it into being. Ellel Grange, a country house just outside the city of Lancaster, provided the first home and the name of Ellel Ministries. Many Christian leaders affirmed the vision and gave it their support. Since then, a hallmark of Peter's ministry has been his willingness to step out in faith to see God move to fulfil His promises, often in remarkable ways.

Under Peter and his wife's leadership, the worldwide teaching and ministry team has seen God move dramatically in many people's lives to bring salvation, hope, healing and deliverance. Together Peter and Fiona teach and minister on many different aspects of healing and discipleship. Ellel Ministries operates by faith and depends on donations and income from training courses to maintain and expand the work.

Outside of Ellel Ministries, Peter was the originator and one of the compilers of the amazingly successful and popular *Mission Praise*, now in its thirtieth anniversary edition (HarperCollins, 2015). It was originally compiled for Billy Graham's Mission England in 1984.

The story of Peter's life and of how God built and extended the ministry is told in his book *Strands of Destiny* (Sovereign World, 2018). He describes many of the extraordinary and miraculous events through which God has sustained the ministry across the years. JOURNEY TO FREEDOM is a culmination of over thirty years of experience teaching the foundational principles of healing and discipleship and ministering to people all over the world.

# ABOUT **ELLEL MINISTRIES** INTERNATIONAL

## Our Vision

Ellel Ministries is a nondenominational Christian mission organization with a vision to equip the Church by welcoming people, teaching them about the Kingdom of God and healing those in need.

## Our Mission

Our mission is to fulfill the above vision throughout the world as God opens the doors, in accordance with the Great Commission of Jesus and the calling of the Church to proclaim the Kingdom of God by preaching the good news, healing the brokenhearted and setting the captives free. We are, therefore, committed to evangelism, healing, deliverance, discipleship and training. The particular Scriptures on which our mission is founded are Luke 9:11; Isaiah 61:1–7; Matthew 28:18–20; Luke 9:1–2; Ephesians 4:12; and 2 Timothy 2:2.

## Our Basis of Faith

God is a Trinity. God the Father loves all people. God the Son, Jesus Christ, is Savior and Healer, Lord and King. God the Holy Spirit indwells Christians and imparts the dynamic power by which they are enabled to continue Christ's ministry. The Bible is the divinely inspired authority in matters of faith, doctrine and conduct and is the basis for teaching.

For further information about Ellel Ministries International, please visit www.ellelministries.org.

# More from
# Peter Horrobin

There are countless moments in our lives when we need wisdom urgently. God has provided the book of Proverbs to give us the baseline we need for clarity. This 40-day devotional, built around key verses in Proverbs, provides a rich source of wisdom to feed the soul and encourage the spirit so you can be empowered to live in the light of heavenly counsel.

*Wisdom from the Proverbs*

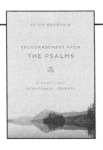

This 40-day journey of faith explores key verses from the Psalms that David recorded during times of distress, joy and triumph. Within these pages, you will find meditations and prayers to anchor these truths into your own life, and spaces to journal what God is speaking to you. Watch His hand in your life on this journey of discovery and transformation!

*Encouragement from the Psalms*

## ✓Chosen